The Bride's Year Ahead

✲✲✲ ✿✿✿

I want to thank all the brides and grooms for allowing me to be a part of their special day. The experience has allowed me the opportunity to share these wonderful photographs with our audience of future brides.

I also want to thank Monica Dietrich, my agent and friend; without her, we would just have pictures.

CAROL ROSS

Published by Sellers Publishing, Inc.

© 2003, 2011, 2017 by PM Design Group, Inc.
Photography © 2003, 2011, 2017 Carol Ross
www.carolrossphotography.com
Additional photo credits on page 272
All rights reserved.

Text by Marguerite Smolen and Claudia Gryvatz Copquin
Cover design by Mary Baldwin & Charlotte Cromwell
Interior design by Charlotte Cromwell

161 John Roberts Rd., South Portland, Maine 04106
Visit our Web site: www.sellerspublishing.com
E-mail: rsp@rsvp.com

ISBN 13: 978-1-4162-4636-7
Library of Congress Control Number: 2017937385

10 9 8 7 6 5 4 3 2 1

Printed in China

The Bride's Year Ahead

≫≫ The Ultimate Month-by-Month Wedding Planner ≪≪

Third Edition

Marguerite Smolen
and Claudia Gryvatz Copquin
PHOTOGRAPHY BY CAROL ROSS

SELLERS
PUBLISHING

❧❧❧ TASKS ❧❧❧

TWELVE MONTHS AHEAD ∽ 10
- ○ Determine who will officiate your wedding
- ○ Set the wedding date
- ○ Create a preliminary guest list
- ○ Book a reception hall
- ○ Book a caterer
- ○ Determine your wedding style

ELEVEN MONTHS AHEAD ∽ 40
- ○ Announce your engagement
- ○ Select invitations and other communication pieces
- ○ Choose your wedding party
- ○ Book a photographer
- ○ Book a videographer

TEN MONTHS AHEAD ∽ 62
- ○ Create your personal improvement plan
- ○ Assemble your experts
- ○ Register for gifts

NINE MONTHS AHEAD ∽ 74
- ○ Choose your wedding theme and decor
- ○ Select music and entertainment

EIGHT MONTHS AHEAD ∽ 90
- ○ Shop for your bridal gown
- ○ Order the gown and schedule fittings
- ○ Shop for wedding party attire
- ○ Choose the groom's attire

SEVEN MONTHS AHEAD ∽ 134
- ○ Make your floral choices
- ○ Shop for wedding cakes
- ○ Select sweets
- ○ Shop for favors

SIX MONTHS AHEAD ∽ 156
- ○ Finalize the guest list
- ○ Plan wedding party events
- ○ Plan toasts

FIVE MONTHS AHEAD ∽ 182
- ○ Plan a honeymoon
- ○ Attend to legal matters
- ○ Attend to business matters

FOUR MONTHS AHEAD ∽ 192
- ○ Secure accommodations for out-of-town guests
- ○ Book wedding day transportation

THREE MONTHS AHEAD ∽ 198
- ○ Choose wedding rings
- ○ Select bridal jewelry
- ○ Mail your invitations
- ○ Learn to dance

TWO MONTHS AHEAD ∽ 212
- ○ Compile your program book
- ○ Plan and book the ceremony rehearsal and dinner
- ○ Keep up with thank you notes

ONE MONTH AHEAD ∽ 238
- ○ Plan your wedding day itinerary
- ○ Organize the reception seating chart
- ○ Apply for a marriage license
- ○ Three weeks ahead up to the the final day of the wedding

❋❋❋ TOOLS ❋❋❋

Introduction

The moment you've dreamed of has finally come. You've found that special someone who loves you just as you are, who will stick with you through good times and bad, now and forever: You're getting married. Of course you want to share your newfound happiness with family and friends, to honor your commitment to join together by planning the celebration of a lifetime. If you're like most engaged couples, though, the prospect of orchestrating such a big event is overwhelming. Wouldn't it be wonderful to have a wedding planner available 24 hours a day to help you prepare for this most important occasion?

Well, now you do. This comprehensive volume is designed with busy couples in mind; it contains all the essential information you need to plan a wedding. Starting with the ceremony, moving on to the reception, and through to the honeymoon, it provides step-by-step instructions on how to create an event that is every bit as unique as the love you share. In the following pages, you'll learn when you should book a reception hall, what questions to ask a caterer, and how to get the most music for your money.

You'll find out how to buy a wedding gown that suits your style and flatters your figure.

We'll help you to personalize your wedding with creative ideas. Check out the floral review section in on pages 139-144 — it features full color photographs of more than 50 popular flowers for bouquets, table decorations, and boutonnieres. And we'll share many of the secrets bridal professionals prefer to keep to themselves.

To make planning your special day both easy and fun, we've broken the whole, complicated process up into simple steps and organized these steps into

a timeline. Each section of this book covers one month in the wedding planning process and opens with a task list for that month. Also included are useful tools — checklists, worksheets, questions-and-answers, and other practical information designed to keep you on track with a minimum of effort.

To make the most of the information contained in this book, skim it first, cover-to-cover. Once you have an overview of the entire planning process, you can get started planning your own wedding by utilizing the information in the first chapter. The book is divided into twelve chapters, because most couples plan their weddings a year in advance. If you have less than a year to plan your celebration, you can combine the activities in multiple months and still have a workable plan — although a somewhat abbreviated one!

Your wedding day should be a fun occasion, providing you with memories to cherish for years to come. *The Bride's Year Ahead* is designed not only to help you to achieve this happy ending, but also to make the months of planning beforehand an enjoyable adventure, too.

Twelve Months Ahead

TASKS:

- ○ Determine who will officiate your wedding
- ○ Set the wedding date
- ○ Create a preliminary guest list
- ○ Book a reception hall
- ○ Book a caterer
- ○ Determine your wedding style
- ○ Prepare an overall estimated budget

TOOLS:

- ○ Questions to Ask an Officiant
- ○ Questions to Ask a Nondenominational Officiant
- ○ Questions to Ask a Reception Hall Vendor and Caterer
- ○ Reception Hall Comparison Worksheet
- ○ Caterer Comparison Worksheet
- ○ Final Reception Hall Choice
- ○ Final Caterer Choice
- ○ Wedding Budget Worksheet

Meet with the Officiant

If both of you are very religious, a meeting with a member of your clergy comes first. As officiant at a sacred event, the priest, minister, or rabbi most likely will have certain constraints regarding the ceremony time and place. These constraints in turn may affect where and when the wedding and reception can be held. In addition, your religion may require that couples complete classes to prepare for marriage. For some religions, it is not unusual for these marriage "prep" classes to take six months or even a year to complete.

 If you are not religious, but consider yourself to be spiritual, you will also want to give some thought to the sacred aspects of a wedding. Do you and your spouse-to-be come from different faiths? Do you need to reconcile any differences? Will you be married in the same faith or by different sets of clergy? You still may want to consider attending some counseling or a marriage-prep course, however, to help make the adjustment to marriage easier in the months after you wed, especially if there are any family issues to discuss or children from a previous marriage.

WHO CAN OFFICIATE AT A WEDDING?

- A justice of the peace, judge, or court clerk who has legal authority to perform marriages officiates at civil weddings.

- A clergy member (priest, minister, or rabbi) conducts religious ceremonies.

- Tribal chiefs officiate at Native American weddings, although the tribe may sometimes grant another person authority to officiate at weddings.

- A friend or family member may be able to officiate at your wedding if the local and state governments allow it. First, check with the agency that issues marriage licenses (often the county clerk) for the location where you are to be married. If allowed, your selected officiant will need to follow the procedure to get ordained online, marry you with a ceremony script that includes a Declaration of Intent, and complete and file the legal marriage certificate. If you select this option for your officiant, the onus is on you and your chosen officiant to do the homework and make sure you follow all the legal procedures.

Nowadays, with so many interfaith and multicultural marriages, it's quite common for couples to desire a secular rather than a religious service. Some couples may wish to have a highly personalized or spiritual wedding ceremony. If you both are okay with being married by a nondenominational minister (there are many who specialize in weddings) or a justice of the peace, you will still need to book the officiant in advance, although maybe not a full twelve months in advance. When searching for a nondenominational officiant, begin by asking friends and relatives for referrals, then search the Internet for officiants in your area. Once you have found a few candidates, the first question to ask is if he or she is legally licensed to perform wedding ceremonies in your state. Next, find out if the officiant has any limitations, in terms of traveling to your desired ceremony location, and if you have a date booked, if the officiant is available.

YOU MAY WANT A NON-DENOMINATIONAL WEDDING IF YOU:

- have no religious affiliation

- want a more personalized ceremony

- would like spiritual/secular values and rituals incorporated into the ceremony

- desire a nonreligious ceremony (but not a civil ceremony)

- would like the ceremony and reception at home, outdoors, or a place where a religious officiant might not want to go

- are a multicultural couple and want elements of both your backgrounds in your ceremony

QUESTIONS TO ASK AN OFFICIANT	NOTES
What is your policy regarding booking a wedding?	
How far in advance should we contact you?	
Are there any required meetings or coursework?	
What is the policy regarding interfaith marriages? Will you officiate together with clergy from another faith?	
What dates and times is the place of worship available?	
Will you officiate in a place other than the place of worship?	
What restrictions does the place of worship have?	
How many people can it hold? Are we allowed to take pictures or to videotape the ceremony? If not, can we take pictures before and after the ceremony?	
Are decorations allowed?	
Is there any restriction on the type of clothing that must be worn? (Some religions may not approve of the current fashion for strapless bridal gowns.) Is there a set ceremony, rite, or ritual that must be followed?	
Can we write our own ceremony or personalize the ceremony in any way?	
Does the place of worship allow outside musicians? Are any restrictions placed on the type of music or number of musicians? Are there any musicians or vocalists available for the ceremony?	
Can guests throw birdseed or rice as the couple exits the premises?	
Is there a room where the bride can dress?	
What is the cost to book the church or synagogue and any of its musicians?	

QUESTIONS TO ASK A NONDENOMINATIONAL OFFICIANT	NOTES
What is your policy regarding booking a wedding?	
How far in advance should we contact you?	
What is the cost for ceremony services?	
Is there an extra fee for the rehearsal?	
How many times will we meet prior to the wedding?	
Are you willing to travel? How far?	
Is there an extra fee for your travel?	
Is there any location where you will not officiate a ceremony?	
Are you available all weekdays, weekends, and holidays?	
How do you customize the ceremony?	
Can we write our own vows?	
Can you include a special reading of our choice?	
How long/short can we make the ceremony?	

Set the Wedding Date

There's a lot to consider when setting the date for your wedding: family, time of year, high season/low season (especially important if you're having a destination wedding), the holidays, even major sporting events. If both of you have your hearts set on a mid-summer wedding with the ceremony Saturday afternoon followed by a Saturday evening reception, plan to book your date early. This choice can be an excellent option; it's a time of year when people expect to attend weddings, guests may find it easier to travel over a weekend, and out-of-town guests can plan on just one overnight. Keep in mind that it's a good idea to not have too much time between the end of the ceremony and the reception; one hour is ideal.

The Thanksgiving holiday presents an opportunity for more time with out-of-town guests and family over the long weekend, as do Columbus Day, the 4th of July, Memorial Day, Labor Day, and even New Year's Eve and Day.

In terms of sporting events, consider the Super Bowl at the end of January/early February, March Madness, golf tournaments, and even college football when selecting a date.

Create a Preliminary Guest List

Once you have cleared the date with the participating clergy (or decided on an option that does not involve an organized religion), your next priority should be to come up with a preliminary guest list. This may seem premature, but in reality, the guest list determines many other early decisions, such as the type of wedding venue you'll need and the budget you'll be working with. Use the Guest List Organizer (see page 162) to note those you'd like to invite knowing that the list may change down the road.

CREATIVE CUISINE

Are you and your fiance foodies? Or maybe you're just not interested in typical wedding fare. It's perfectly acceptable to think outside the standard "chicken-or-fish" sit-down menu when hiring a caterer or planning how to feed your guests and yourselves on your wedding day. First, make sure your reception vendor allows outside catering. If so, here are some fresh ideas for food at your wedding:

- **food trucks:** a favorite food truck for something special, or multiple food trucks for a full smorgasbord

- **food stations:** a variety of food to keep every guest happy

- **barbeque:** mouth-watering burgers, ribs, and grilled vegetables and sides

- **pig or turkey roast**

- **picnic fare:** gourmet sandwiches, slaws, potato chips, lemonade, homemade cookies and fruit pie

- **build-your-own taco bar:** seasoned beef, fish, and veggie tacos with all the fixings, even a separate salsa bar, can be a fun, money-saving approach

- **pizza station:** elevate the standard pizza with unusual or decadent toppings

- **brunch buffet:** an omelet station, a waffle bar, sizzling bacon, warm buttered biscuits and toast, a pastry table, mimosas, a coffee bar, and more

- **cocktails and passable appetizers only**

- **salty and sweet snack table and local microbrew samplings:** a variety of gourmet popcorn, nut mixes, granola bars, chips, pretzels, and more with a side of microbrews

The ideas are endless, so think about your favorite food and have fun brainstorming the best way to enjoy it at your wedding!

Book a Reception Hall and a Caterer

If you're like most couples, the majority of your budget will be spent on the reception. So, this month, you will make visiting reception halls and caterers a priority. Another reason for making the reception this month's priority is that, generally speaking, you will have to work quickly to book a reception hall or caterer, especially if you are thinking of a venue that is very popular. Most banquet halls and hotels are booked a year in advance, especially during the most popular months for weddings (spring, summer, and early fall in most parts of the country). Booking a venue now is particularly important if both of you are set on a specific date for your wedding. It's true that many couples want their wedding date to be significant — for example, the date of your first kiss or first date. However, it's also a reality that just as often the venue of your dreams is booked on that special date, leading to disappointment. So do have a few alternate dates in mind when booking the hall, and try to be flexible. Of course, if you are working two or more years in advance, then you can likely hit upon your preferred wedding date and take your pick of the most popular venues in your area.

Use the worksheets in this chapter to make a careful comparison of each of the venues before deciding which one you will book. In addition, you may want to consult with an experienced event and/ or wedding planner who can offer guidance in regard to the best venues that would suit your needs and desires. The planner might also work with you on your budget and later on provide you with ideas and resources for the reception.

QUESTIONS TO ASK A RECEPTION HALL VENDOR AND CATERER	VENDOR #1
What is the maximum number of guests a room can hold for a sit-down meal? For a buffet? For cocktails and hors d'oeuvres?	
How many wedding receptions do you cater in the same time period? Will our wedding party have exclusive use of your facility?	
Is alcohol allowed? If so, is it BYOB or must it be purchased through the facility? Does the facility offer a five- or four-hour open bar?	
Is a champagne (or sparkling wine) toast included in the price?	
Is a wedding cake included in the price? Can I order my cake elsewhere?	
How many hors d'oeuvres do you make for each guest? How many different varieties of hors d'oeuvres are included in the price?	
Can I have a cupcake tower, cookie station, or chocolate fountain?	
What type of coffee service is provided?	
Are personnel charges included (for waitstaff, bartenders, maître d', master of ceremonies, wedding planner)?	
Is there a coat check?	
What type of service do you supply (for example: French-plated tableside; American-plated in the kitchen and brought to the table; ultra-class French-prepared and plated within view)?	
Is valet parking available?	
Do you offer a bridal hospitality room, in which the wedding party may freshen up, or overnight bridal couple accommodations?	
Are flowers included? Is there a house florist, or may I bring my own floral arrangements?	
When is the deposit due?	
When is the balance due?	
Are taxes and gratuities included in the fee?	
What are your overtime charges and how can they be avoided?	
Is liability insurance available?	
What is your cancellation policy? Is cancellation insurance available?	

VENDOR #2	VENDOR #3

Don't forget – get all costs in writing and read any contract carefully before signing it.
Better yet, have an unemotional, detached (but trustworthy) third-party read the contracts for you.

RECEPTION HALL COMPARISON WORKSHEET

RECEPTION HALL NAME AND ADDRESS	CONTACT NAME, PHONE NUMBER, WEB SITE AND EMAIL	GUEST CAPACITY	PRICE RANGE PER GUEST (minimum/ maximum)	TYPE OF PACKAGE (e.g., 5-course sit-down, food stations, buffet)

SEPARATE ROOM FOR COCKTAILS?	RATIO OF SERVERS TO GUESTS	DATES AND TIMES AVAILABLE	CEREMONY FACILITY	DEPOSIT

NOTES

_____

_____

_____

_____

_____

_____

_____

_____

_____

_____

_____

_____

CATERER COMPARISON WORKSHEET

CATERER NAME AND ADDRESS	CONTACT NAME, PHONE NUMBER, WEB SITE AND EMAIL	PRICE RANGE (minimum/ maximum)	PROVIDES TABLES, CHAIRS, LINENS ETC.	TYPE OF PACKAGE (e.g., 5-course sit-down, food stations, buffet)

COCKTAILS	SPECIALIZE IN CERTAIN TYPES OF FOOD?	RATIO OF SERVERS TO GUESTS	DO YOU HAVE A LICENSE, LIABILITY, INSURANCE, ETC?	DATES AND TIMES AVAILABLE	DEPOSIT

NOTES

_____

_____

_____

_____

_____

_____

_____

_____

_____

_____

_____

FINAL RECEPTION HALL CHOICE

NAME	CONTACT PERSON	ADDRESS, TELEPHONE, EMAIL	OTHER

FINAL CATERER CHOICE

NAME	CONTACT PERSON	ADDRESS, TELEPHONE, EMAIL	OTHER

COST	DEPOSIT/DATE	PRELIMINARY GUEST COUNT	BALANCE DUE	OTHER

COST	DEPOSIT/DATE	PRELIMINARY GUEST COUNT	BALANCE DUE	OTHER

NOTES

_____
_____
_____
_____
_____
_____
_____
_____

PROFESSIONAL WEDDING PLANNERS

Hiring a wedding planner is not on every couple's list of priorities, especially as this is an added expense to the overall wedding budget. However, there are numerous benefits to having a professional by your side. A wedding planner can do much of the legwork for you in terms of narrowing your vendor options. She'll ask you for your overall vision, number of guests, and budget, and then provide you with recommendations for the venue, florist, entertainment, and other vendors. Different wedding planners offer varying levels of service, but generally, a planner can:

- book appointments for you

- visit vendors with you

- assist in decision-making

- remind you of deposit deadlines

- review contracts with you

- negotiate prices

- offer ideas for decor and other details

- be on site the day of the wedding to ensure all goes as it should

Expect to spend about 10 to 15 percent of your total budget for full wedding planning. It's perfectly acceptable to ask for consultations, usually an hour or so, if you only want advice and referrals for a specific aspect of your wedding. Or you can hire a consultant to coordinate just the actual wedding day.

Determine Your Wedding Style

Of course, you can mix and mingle wedding styles. But for those couples who don't know what kind of wedding they want, here are some ideas for finding a style.

Country: Held outdoors in a rural environment or in a summerhouse; underneath a rose-covered arch or gazebo; or indoors in a barn, cabin, or rustic country house; buckets filled with wildflowers; a horse-drawn cart; barbecue or farm-grown, organic picnic fare. The bride will wear a mid-calf or ankle-length dress without a train and one floral hairpin or floral wreath. The maids will wear print or simple cotton or linen dresses. The groom will wear a suit or jacket and tie with brown or gray trousers.

Historic/Theme: Popular ideas include Victorian, Civil War, Wild West, Maritime, Medieval, and Broadway musicals such as *The Phantom of the Opera* — but your imagination can only add to the list! Once you've decided on a theme, you can recreate it in as much or as little detail as you wish — down to dressing in costume and serving food based on historic menus. Many outfits cater to costuming wedding parties.

Urban Sophisticate: Elegant big-city hotel or loft wedding characterized by formal linens; an open bar with a four- or five-course meal; floral "trees" or "towers" on the tables, allowing people to see each other through the super-tall glass or acrylic vases or pedestals; and big band or orchestral dance music. The bride might wear a gown with a long train for the ceremony, and an altogether different gown for the reception, while her groom (and any male guests) may wear white or black tie. The bridesmaids often wear black cocktail dresses.

Avant-garde: Held in a museum, warehouse, or other artistic venue, this wedding will feature theatrical set decorations, strolling performers for entertainment, and a buffet or variety of food stations providing diverse fare. Everyone dresses creatively!

Clubby: Celebrate your wedding in exclusive surrounds on a small scale at a club in town. You might belong to one or can access a private club that rents to outsiders — a women's, art, or some other social club. The atmosphere is more like someone's home than a standard banquet hall. You can personalize it — but still keep a traditional flavor. The groom wears a traditional morning coat

START YOUR DREAM BOARD

A wedding dream board (or vision board) is the place where you collect wedding-related images that showcase ideas that you'd like to incorporate into your wedding While some couples have binders full of notes and pages torn from magazines, others may use a physical cork board and thumbtacks to highlight their ideas. Most dream boards now, are created and kept online using Pinterest or other online site. It is best to start this process early as a way to envision everything from the setting and venue to the tiniest details, and ultimately, your overall wedding style.

Consider having vision boards (or files) for the following categories:

- Announcements/invitations
- Attire
- Hair and makeup
- Flowers
- Venue
- Color palette
- Food
- Cakes
- Music/playlists
- Photography & videography style
- Favors
- DIY
- Special details

or a navy blue blazer with gray pants, white shirt, and tie, and the bride wears a semiformal dress. If the groom is in the military, he may wear his dress uniform.

Ethnic: Celebrate diversity in a museum or other location that captures your heritage. Your food, attire, and decor will be informed by the traditions of your culture. Guests will treasure this opportunity to feast their senses on the flavors and atmosphere of a remote place or time. If you incorporate several traditions into your celebration, you can make it a true multicultural event!

Traditional: At a catering hall or country club. Mom and Dad's generation will happily dig into the prime rib, and you'll be able to get linens in your "wedding

SMALL, INTIMATE WEDDINGS

There are a number of reasons why you may want to forgo a large-scale, lavish wedding and instead host an intimate affair. The largest portion of your wedding budget will go towards the venue rental, food, and beverages, with the fees calculated on a per person basis. So the greater number of guests, the larger the final bill. Couples who have limited funds, therefore, should not hesitate to host a small-scale wedding, which will be much more affordable than one for guests of one hundred and over. But money may not be the only motivation. Perhaps you are a couple who doesn't have a large, extended family. You may want a wedding that is quite informal (in which case, a restaurant would be the perfect venue). Privacy is another reason why you might opt for a small wedding — it's perfectly acceptable to have a desire to share this occasion with a limited number of close-knit friends and relatives. Second weddings are often not grand and elaborate, merely because couples have already been there, done that! In addition, you may want to include all of your guests somehow in every aspect of this celebration, and that would be almost impossible in a large reception.

In regards to planning an intimate wedding, you will still need many of the basic elements — you'll want to wear a wedding gown (perhaps one that isn't quite that formal), have a photographer and videographer on hand, and offer entertainment so guests can dance and have a fun time at this special celebration. Regardless of the size and scope of the wedding, what makes for a memorable day is the love and joy surrounding you.

colors." The pace is pleasingly predictable, the atmosphere is chaste and romantic, and the clockwork efficiency of an experienced staff (perhaps one that has watched you grow up) ensures that everyone attending will have a good time. The bride will wear a traditional white wedding gown with a chapel train, the groom will wear a tuxedo, and the bridesmaids will wear dresses to match the table linens.

Garden: Your family's backyard sets the stage for a casual, midday reception. Loads of spring flowers spruce up the rented tent, creating a fresh, colorful ambience. In keeping with the informal theme, the bride wears a white tea-length dress, with a touch of accent color. Bridesmaids wear matching colors but not matching dresses. An elegant luncheon buffet includes delicate tea sandwiches, crudités, and pastries, and the bride and groom offer guests a one-of-a-kind custom cocktail created just for this occasion.

Destination/Beach: In addition to the couple, the sand and sea are the stars here. A simple, cotton canopy is set up oceanside for the ceremony, which is preferably just around sunset. No high heels allowed — the bride wears an informal cotton dress, while the groom sports a relaxed, button-down white shirt and matching slacks. For entertainment, Caribbean music or a reggae band add a fun and festive touch to the romantic, moonlit setting. As for fare: it's all seafood.

New Ways to Wed

Many couples today realize that weddings are a wonderful opportunity to gather all of the key people in their lives for one meaningful celebration. If a one-day celebration just doesn't seem like enough quality time with friends and relatives, consider a wedding that incorporates additional social gatherings either before or after the wedding.

The weekend wedding: Plan a long weekend that's chock-full of fun celebrations. Along with the standard wedding-related events, consider an additional brunch for out-of-towners, a casual barbecue and outdoor games, or a group sightseeing excursion.

The all-night wedding: Instead of disappearing after the reception, plan an after-party at a nearby location (e.g., a local pub or a pool paty at the hotel). While not all your guests will be up for the all-nighter, it can be a fun party-extension for those who are.

The family reunion wedding: While most weddings are in part family reunion, you may choose to further embrace this aspect of your family gathering. If you plan your wedding to coincide with a major family occasion (e.g., a great-grandmother's milestone birthday or a silver anniversary), you have that much more to celebrate. You can incorporate family photos, videos, toasts, and tributes into your wedding that will increase the family celebration many-fold.

The destination wedding: If many of your guests will need to fly into town for your nuptials, why not make their vacation time and expenses really worth it. Plan your wedding in an exotic location and your guests can enjoy your wedding and a bit of paradise. (Note that this can be an expensive option for your guests — especially if you are getting married somewhere during its high tourist season — and so your guest list may fall short of your expectations.)

The progressive wedding: If you grew up in New York City but live in Chicago, and your fiancé hails from San Francisco, where do you tie the knot? You can turn your wedding into a multi-city event. Have a prenuptial cocktail party in New York. Have your formal wedding in Chicago. Then have a post-wedding (or post honeymoon) celebration in San Francisco. You can get everyone involved and have special memories from town to town or coast to coast.

The surprise wedding: This is a wedding disguised as a "regular" party. You and your fiancé invite guests to an incredible party. Then, mid-evening, slip away to don your wedding gown and formal wear, and return to announce that a wedding will take place! Shy couples will love the immediacy and simplicity of this event — which fast forwards through all the pre-wedding parties and goes directly to the main event.

THE PROS AND CONS OF AN OUTDOOR WEDDING

If you're a couple who thrives in the outdoors, you might be dreaming of tying the knot in a local park, on a beach, or in a nature preserve. And that's a perfectly fine idea, as long as you are fully aware of the pros and cons of such an undertaking. Among the pros: the opportunity for spectacular photos within the elements (sunsets, water, trees, blooming flowers). Among the cons: unpredictable weather could wreak havoc on your day.

When considering an outdoor wedding, think about whether you want both the ceremony and the reception outside. If your heart is set on a full-blown al fresco wedding and you have located the perfect spot for it (a local beach or park), inquire about tent rentals, just in case of inclement weather. You will also likely need a few permits. Contact your town or village hall to inquire about this, as well as about parking facilities, restrooms, food and alcohol consumption, and cleanup. You'll also need to rent tables and chairs, and set up electric outlets and lighting equipment. This will require quite a lot of work on your part. A more practical option might be to break the day down by having the ceremony at an outdoor location followed by an indoor reception. You can accomplish this by booking a venue that has both beautiful grounds for exchanging vows (often romantic gazebos are available) and indoor banquet rooms for the festivities. The weather permitting, you and your guests can wander in and out in this type of facility, pleasing everyone involved. Consider booking an inn or a lodge (especially if yours is a smaller wedding), one where you have an option of an outdoor ceremony and even reception; plus your guests can book rooms there.

Now is also the time to consider general guidelines for the type of wedding you want to have. Deciding on the type of wedding is important because it will help to focus your resources, thus allowing more time to investigate possibilities that are realistic for you. Figuring out the total dollar amount you can spend for your big day will save you time for the same reason. Venues and service providers that exceed your budget can be eliminated quickly, leaving more time for careful shopping among those who are within your means.

Don't worry about making a detailed spending plan for every item just yet. For now, just determine a total dollar cost. You will not be able to identify an allowance for an item until you have shopped around a bit. As you start to compare prices during this first month, you will begin to refine your priorities. By month's end, you should have a good idea of how much you will spend on each aspect of the wedding. Until then, we suggest using a pencil to fill out the budget worksheet on pages 38-39.

SAVE MONEY ON YOUR RECEPTION BY:

- Limiting the guest list to 40 people or fewer. A smaller reception will allow you to choose from among many more places, and makes possible intimate (less expensive) venues, such as local restaurants and bed-and-breakfasts.
- Getting married on a weekday. Keep in mind that work obligations may prevent some guests from sharing in your celebration. If this is unacceptable to you, then a weekend wedding makes better sense.
- Choosing a less popular time and day, if you decide to hold the wedding on a weekend. Saturday nights tend to be most popular, followed by Saturday afternoons.
- A wedding breakfast or brunch is not as popular as an evening dinner and reception, but can still be quite lovely. Sunday is typically less popular than Saturdays, if only because most people need to get back to work on Monday.
- Getting married during a time of year that is not especially in demand. For example, most reception halls are looking for business in late January and early February (which is one reason so many bridal shows are held in those months).
- Booking a facility that has not yet opened or has been opened for only a short time. New businesses may have openings to fill and a reputation to establish.

WEDDING BUDGET WORKSHEET

Creating an estimated budget is crucial to the planning of your wedding. Throughout the book are a multitude of helpful expense worksheets for everything from flower costs to your honeymoon. As decisions get made, combine the final amounts and dates to pay in the master at-a-glance financial overview at the end of the book (see page 260).

ITEM	COST	DUE DATES
Engagement party		
Engagement photograph		
REHEARSAL DINNER		
Site		
Food and service		
Liquor		
Entertainment		
Other		
Transportation to rehearsal dinner		
Attendants' gifts		
CEREMONY		
Site		
Officiant		
Decorations		
Flowers		
Music		
Service assistance		
Day-of assistant		
Photographer		
Videographer		
Programs/pew cards		
Professional wedding planner		
Certificate		
Registration fee		
Birdseed/favors		
Transportation to ceremony		
Bridal flowers		
Wedding party flowers		

ITEM	COST	DUE DATES
CEREMONY CONT.		
Groom and groomsmen flowers		
Parents of bride and groom flowers		
Programs/pew cards		
Bridal gown		
Tuxedo		
Bridesmaids' dresses		
Groomsmen attire		
COCKTAIL PARTY		
Food and service		
Liquor		
Entertainment		
Decor		
Flowers		
Transportation to cocktail party		
RECEPTION		
Site		
Food and service		
Liquor		
Decor		
Flowers		
Favors & Gifts		
Wedding cake		
Viennese pastry table		
Valet parking		
Transportation to reception		
Photography		
Videography		
Entertainment		
End of reception outfit		
HONEYMOON		

Eleven Months Ahead

TASKS:

- ○ Announce your engagement
- ○ Select invitations and other communication pieces
- ○ Choose your wedding party
- ○ Book a photographer
- ○ Book a videographer

TOOLS:

- ○ Invitation Worksheet
- ○ Wedding Attendants and Participants and their Duties
- ○ Wedding Photography and Videography Checklist
- ○ Wedding Photography Estimates
- ○ Wedding Videography Estimates

Announce Your Engagment

Announcing your engagement formally in the local newspaper was a common wedding tradition until somewhat recently. While this is still done in certain regions and in some local papers (often for a fee), many couples forego this traditional approach to announcing their engagement and make their grand announcement on social media or in a more personal way. You may want the keepsake of a newspaper announcement, or you may have too geographically wide a network to make a local newspaper announcement meaningful to you.

However you choose to announce to the world that you are engaged, you'll want to let those closest to you (parents, close family, and friends) know the good news first. If you choose to skip the formal announcement now, you can consider submitting a post-nuptial notice to your local newspaper soon after the wedding. If you plan to submit information to a newspaper, check the newspaper's Web site for information about word count, standard language, and photo specifications before submitting your announcement.

Invitations, and Other Communication Necessities

Paper, typeface, and ink color all reflect your personality and set the tone for your wedding. If your invitation is formal, guests will expect your wedding to be formal. If you send an invitation that has a more colorful and whimsical feeling, guests will expect that lighthearted spirit to be reflected on your wedding day.

When selecting your stationery products — invitations, thank-you cards, place cards, ceremony program, and menu — keep your theme consistent. Everything should match or coordinate These days, thanks to the Internet, couples can count on a myriad of options in terms of style, design, and size. Ordering online can facilitate the process, but you do have to be very careful, as you'll be working without guidance from a live expert. If you are uncertain about what you want, it's best to consult with a wedding invitation expert in your area. They can guide you in making the best choices, and ordering exactly what you want. Printing errors will be easier to rectify when working with a local vendor rather than the Internet, as well.

Going Digital

Wedding Web sites and wedding-related e-stationery are becoming increasingly popular with today's brides and grooms for many reasons. Online options are less expensive, more environmentally friendly, and often more customizable than print-on-paper options. Although the most formal and traditional weddings still call for print-on-paper, mailed invitations and other wedding stationery, it is advisable for many couples to consider at least some of the digital options available. You may want traditional printed invitations, but still need a wedding Web site to showcase photos, maps of the area and hotel information for out-of-town guests, registry information (including links), and more. You may find that some of your stationery needs are better as e-vites while others require printed cards. Explore all the options before deciding what works best for your special day and all the events leading up to it.

There are numerous options available for couples who wish to create a wedding Web site. Many are free; others charge a monthly or yearly fee. Before you decide which service to use, think about what you want and need your Web site to communicate to your guests. Some sites are better at showcasing photos.

Others allow you lots of ways customize the look of the site. Because the options are ever-evolving, you should look at multiple sites and their offerings, and then read reviews of the site before making your selection. Wedding Web sites can be loads of fun to create as well as an incredibly useful way to compile and detail information for you and your guests.

There are many and ever-expanding online options for both printed and e-stationery, with some Web sites offering both, allowing you to keep the look of your invitations consistent in both digital and print form. The individual stationery pieces are often highly customizable, with a wide variety of easy-to-use templates, photo and art upload options, designer artwork, suggested

BRUSH UP ON YOUR STATIONERY VOCABULARY

Engraving was invented in the seventeenth century as an easy way to reproduce documents that monks had formerly penned by hand. An engraver cuts an image in reverse into a copper plate or steel die. The die is then used to impress paper with ink. The resulting type feels sharp to the touch. Today only invitations for the most formal weddings are engraved, traditionally with a simple Roman script on 100% cotton fiber paper.

Thermography was designed to look like engraving. The process uses a paper plate with an aluminum backing to chemically transfer an image of the lettering on paper. Resinous powder is then applied to the wet ink. As heat melts the powder, it sticks to the ink and raises the lettering. The paper itself remains flat. Although it is raised lettering, it is not as sharp as engraving. However, it is much less expensive.

Calligraphy is still hand-penned by artists, as it has been for centuries, using black or colored ink in copperplate or italic lettering. The fanciest calligraphy styles have additional embellishments, such as handpainted roses, or ornamental flourishes reminiscent of the folk art.

Chancery-style lettering, similar to that found on the Declaration of Independence, is popular, not just because it is endorsed by tradition, but also because it uses little space.

wordings, and more. You may want some of your stationery printed while other pieces work better as digital cards. Consider all your stationery needs, then determine which e-vite site offers everything you want. Many wedding-specific e-vite sites not only help you create beautiful invitations and other "paper" necessities, but they also offer simple and handy ways to link to your registry and track RSVPs.

Tips for Choosing Print Stationery

Compare styles, sizes, price ranges, and delivery schedules for invitations and other paper goods before making your decision. Consider postage, as well, when selecting size and paper stock.

Custom invitations ordered from manufacturers have different delivery times — some at four weeks, some at six weeks. Shop early enough so ordering time docs not limit your selection.

You can also choose from a range of do-it-yourself invitations from an office supply store, art supply store, or stationer — you may be surprised by the creative options that are available! These can be run through your home laser or inkjet printer.

If you have some time (and patience), you can emboss store-bought invitations one-by-one with gold foil.

Invitations consisting of a translucent piece of paper on top of heavier stock fastened at the top with a ribbon are a popular option. These also can be found in do-it-yourself supply stores.

Couples celebrating in a traditional manner tend to use shades of white or off-white, but couples who choose a different path are increasingly sending out boldly colored invitations that often reflect the wedding color scheme.

STATIONERY ETIQUETTE

Traditional etiquette decreed it acceptable to include the reception invitation at the bottom of the ceremony invitation, along with the notation, "Please respond." Response cards and a self-addressed, stamped envelope are new customs that have developed over the past couple of decades. Addressing envelopes by hand saves the cost of calligraphy or printing and adds a personal touch to your invitation.

With all the care and thought you've given to your wedding plans, it follows that you want the invitations to deliver your announcement clearly and properly. We present several examples of formats from traditional — with the bride's parents hosting — to contemporary and less formal celebrations where the couple hosts. Forms of address also fall under categories of formal vs. less so, and we include suggestions for both.

Formal/Traditional: Mr., Mrs., Ms., etc., are fine to use. In cases where the title is something else, for instance Doctor, the parent who has the title goes first: Doctor Joanne Smith and Mr. James T. Smith or Doctor and Mrs. James T. Smith.

Nontraditional: The courtesy titles may be dropped altogether and it's not unusual to use first names.

INVITATION WORKSHEET

Supplier Name:		Phone no:			
Address:		E-mail:			
		Web site:			

Item:	Description:	Cost:	Order Date:	Deposit:	Balance Due:

Supplier Name:		Phone no:			
Address:		E-mail:			
		Web site:			

Item:	Description:	Cost:	Order Date:	Deposit:	Balance Due:

SAMPLE WEDDING INVITATION WORDING

If married parents have the same surname, the form of address is traditional and names are fully spelled out. If the married parents have different surnames, the woman's name is placed first and styled as in the second example.

Mr. and Mrs. James Thomas Smith
request the pleasure of your company at the marriage ceremony
of their daughter Melody Joanne Smith to Samuel Patton Jones

Ms. Joanne Park and Mr. James Thomas Smith
request the pleasure of your company at the marriage ceremony
of their daughter Melody Joanne Smith to Samuel Patton Jones

If the parents are divorced, and she retains her married name, their names are listed on two lines with the woman's name first. Omit the "and" between names.

Mrs. Joanne Smith
Mr. James Thomas Smith
request the pleasure of your company at the marriage ceremony
of their daughter Melody Joanne Smith to Samuel Patton Jones

If the parents are divorced, and they remarry, and she retains her married name, her name along with her new husband are listed on one line with the birth parent's name first.

Ms. Joanne Smith and Mr. Edward White
Mr. James Thomas Smith and Ms. Eloise Stone
request the pleasure of your company at the marriage ceremony
of their daughter Melody Joanne Smith to Samuel Patton Jones

If a parent is deceased, it is not necessary to include the name, but many couples feel strongly about doing so. A suggested phrasing may be:

You are invited to share in the joy of the marriage of
Melody Joanne Smith, daughter of James Thomas Smith
and the late Joanne Smith, to Samuel Patton Jones

If the couple plans to host, there really isn't a right way or a wrong way. Generally, courtesy titles are omitted, the couple's name appears first, and the bride-to-be's name leads.

Melody Joanne Smith and Samuel Patton Jones
together with their parents (or families) invite you to share . . .

Choose Your Wedding Party

Close on the heels of your engagement announcement, you'll be expected to announce the members of your bridal party. It's actually a good idea to give some thought to who you would like to be involved before you announce your engagement, since this question almost invariably arises once your plans and wedding date have been mentioned.

Traditionally, the maid of honor is female, but it's not uncommon for contemporary brides to reserve this spot for their "male of honor," "man of honor," or "honor attendant" if their best friend happens to be a guy. In keeping with today's focus on personalizing weddings, the best man these days can even be man's best friend — a beloved dog. Couples embarking on their second weddings might opt to include only their children in the bridal party.

Traditionally, the size of the wedding party should logically reflect the type of wedding you are having. For instance, an intimate wedding with only fifty guests calls for a maid of honor and one or two bridesmaids, tops. You don't want half of the wedding guest list to be in the bridal party, in other words. In addition, when selecting bridemaids, consider logistics such as residence: If one or more of them live far away from you, will they have access to a qualified seamstress for gown fittings? Will they be able to attend the bridal shower, bachelorette party, and rehearsal dinner? If not, will this create hurt feelings? The same considerations should be given to the best man and groomsmen.

WEDDING ATTENDANTS AND PARTICIPANTS AND THEIR DUTIES

TITLE	DUTIES
Maid/matron of honor *Sister or close friend;* *may have both*	**AT CEREMONY** • Prior to ceremony, help the bride get dressed • Precede the bride, as well as flower girl and ring bearer, down the aisle • Arrange bride's train and veil after the bride walks down the aisle and before ceremony • Hold groom's wedding band during ceremony • During vows and exchange of rings, hold the bride's bouquet • Straighten bride's train and, with best man, follow couple down the aisle after ceremony • Sign marriage certificate as a witness **AT RECEPTION** • Accompany bride and groom for pictures • Arrange bride's bustle and veil prior to reception entrance • Stand in the receiving line • Sit at the head table to the groom's left • Toast the couple • Dance with best man during the formal dance introducing wedding party **AFTERWARDS** • Help bride change for honeymoon • Help keep track of gifts
Bridesmaid *Bride's close friend,* *sister of groom, younger* *female family member or* *relative; may have* *more than one*	**AT CEREMONY** • Assist with last-minute preparations • Help keep track of belongings in dressing room • Receive bouquet at bride's house and help florist pass out flowers • Follow flower girl/ring bearer and precede maid of honor down the aisle at the start of ceremony • Accompanied by groomsman, follow maid of honor down the aisle after ceremony • Accompany bride and groom for pictures **AT RECEPTION** • Stand in the receiving line next to the maid of honor • Sit at either end of the head table next to assigned groomsman • Dance with groomsman during the formal dance introducing wedding party
Flower girl *Young female child*	**AT CEREMONY** • Proceed bride and her father during processional • May stand at altar or sit in bride's mother's pew just before reaching the altar • Follow bride and groom during recessional • Carry basket of petals and scatter them on the aisle runner • Accompany bride and groom for pictures

TITLE	DUTIES
Best man *Groom's brother or best friend*	**AT CEREMONY** • Coordinate transportation • Organize ushers • Act as groom's valet • Stand next to groom during ceremony • Hold bride's wedding band during ceremony • Together with maid of honor, exit down the aisle after ceremony • Hold clergy and ceremony fees and cash for tipping • Sign marriage certificate as a witness **AT RECEPTION** • Accompany bride and groom for pictures • Traditionally, you do not stand in the receiving line (although this custom is changing) • Sit at the head table to the bride's right • Gives first toast to the bride • During the first dance, dance with maid of honor **AFTERWARDS** • Organizes keys, luggage, and getaway • After the wedding, return groom's tuxedo or other rentals
Groomsman/usher *Groom's close friend, brother, relative*	**AT CEREMONY** • Assist with last-minute preparations • Review seating areas for special guests • Seat guests appropriately upon arrival (bride's guests to the left, groom's guests to the right) • Offer arm when seating single female guests • Seat bride's mother in first pew on left and seat groom's mother in first pew on right • Lay aisle runner and loop ribbons over pews • Proceed up the aisle in pairs prior to processional • Stand next to best man at the altar • Escort bridesmaid down aisle during recessional (follow maid of honor and best man) • Remove pew ribbons and roll up aisle runner • Accompany bride and groom for pictures **AT THE RECEPTION** • Sit at either end of the head table next to assigned bridesmaid • Dance with bridesmaid during the formal dance introducing wedding party
Ring bearer *Young male child*	**AT CEREMONY** • Carry bride's wedding band (or a symbolic ring) on a pillow down the aisle • Precede flower girl(s) and bride and her father during processional • May stand at altar or sit in bride's mother's pew just before reaching the altar • Remain seated during recessional • Accompany bride and groom for pictures

Wedding Photography

Few aspects of a wedding incite more emotion than wedding photos. They are a permanent record of one of life's most important milestones. With technological developments, the wedding photography industry is rapidly evolving. Photographers have different shooting styles and different ways they approach weddings, so when reviewing possible photographers, be sure to ask about their approach and view several recent wedding portfolios. Do you like the documentary style or the more traditional posed style. Perhaps a fine art approach is more what you're looking for. Most photographers will have lots of information on their Web sites, including a portfolio, a Q&A section, and at least some basic information about their standard wedding package. Make sure you know what is included in each photographer's wedding package before you sign on the dotted line.

Most photographers will offer a basic wedding package that includes one photographer for a set amount of time. The package should state a specific amount of time, with a clear rate for additional hours, or a specific list of the wedding events they will shoot. Some photographers may work with, or offer for an additional fee, a second shooter with whom they work in tandem. You don't really need to know what brands of cameras your photographer is planning to use, but you should know if they are shooting film or digital. Ask photographers who you are considering what they shoot and why.

For digital photography, the package should include a private (password protected), online gallery of edited digital images. Ask how long after the wedding you can expect to see your photos — the turnaround is much quicker with digital photographers. You, and those you share the password with, are often invited to order (for an additional charge) high-quality prints, specialty prints, and other items showcasing your selected images. You will likely also receive a flash (USB) drive with the edited, high-resolution images. Your photographer may also put together a high-quality printed and bound wedding album. There are many great and ever-evolving options, so be sure you understand what you are paying for up front, what the add-on options are, and what they cost.

Some couples still opt for film photography because they like the look or the approach. This can certainly lead to beautiful photographs, but you may pay a higher fee and perhaps have fewer photos in the end. Because film photographers don't have the option of reviewing photos as they go, some consider film photography more risky than digital photography. As with any photographer, find out what their standard package includes and what is available for additional fees.

A CAMERA IN EVERY POCKET

Most people, including wedding guests, rarely, if ever, leave home without their cell phones. This can be a photography boom or bust, depending on your approach to photographing your wedding. Some couples used to purchase disposable cameras for reception tables, and encourage guests to snap away throughout the reception. Couples would then collect the disposable cameras at the end of the reception, develop the film, and have a bounty of memories from their guests' point of view. That same approach is made easier today by encouraging your guests to snap away with their cell phones, and then post the pictures to various social media using your pre-designated wedding #. Make sure your wedding # is unique and that you let all your guests know exactly what it is, then have fun looking at everyone's posts whenever you're ready to log into social media and revisit your big day.

However, some couples want to leave the photographic documentation up to the professionals and would rather not have cell phones obstructing views throughout their event. It can be frustrating to see your professional wedding photos showcasing your guests taking photos or filming instead of fully enjoying the moment! If this might cause a problem for you, it's important to let guests know when it is and isn't okay to snap away. A simple announcement by the M.C. at the beginning of your reception, or a note in the program should do the trick.

A fun way to let your guests play with photos without having cell phones take over is to have a photo booth at your wedding reception. Photo booths are becoming more high-style and can be prettied up for a wedding. Printed photo booth strips make a fun souvenir for your guests and there's often a copy of each photo strip for the wedding couple, too.

Once you've decided on your photographer and know that he or she is available for your wedding date, get a written contract and payment plan with at least two, ideally three, installments. If you are working with a photography agency, specify the name of the photographer on the contract, so you are sure to see the person you've discussed your wedding with on your wedding day. You don't want a last-minute substitute you've never met and who doesn't know your wishes.

Wedding Videography

We've all heard couples lament that their wedding day was a blur — so many people and so much excitement and emotion all packed into one day. How could you possibly remember every detail and moment? Hiring a wedding videographer is the best way to capture your wedding day story. No longer is wedding videography a single, obtrusive camera on a stationary tripod capturing your day in real (and often painfully slow) time. Today's wedding videography is all about telling a story, capturing key moments (even those you didn't know were happening on the day!), and evoking the overall feeling of your special day with creative cinematography. As with wedding photography, there are several different styles and approaches to filming your wedding, so put the same care and effort into your research. What approach best suits you as a couple? Do you prefer a highlights video with a special song playing over the full video, or do you wish to hear all the speeches and guest commentary mixed throughout your film? From artsy to dramatic to flirty, make sure you determine what you want and then find the right videographer for your style and sensibilities.

Before signing a contract, it's important to understand what you are paying for. What can you expect for your final, edited video? How many hours will they film? How many cameras and videographers will be at your wedding. How and when will they deliver your wedding video to you? What do they consider standard and what will cost extra? Do they have any special equipment such as an old-fashioned Super-8 camera or drone capabilities? Determine how much of the pre-wedding activities you would like professionally filmed, if any. Get a written contract and a clear payment plan with two or three payment installments.

WEDDING PHOTOGRAPHY & VIDEOGRAPHY CHECKLIST

Most photographers offer a variety of wedding photography packages. It is important to provide your photographer with a list of the events and people you want photographed or filmed. Use this list of standard wedding photo opportunities to compile your own.

Formal Portraits
- ○ Full-length bridal portrait in studio
- ○ Close-up bridal portrait
- ○ Full-length couple portrait in studio
- ○ Close-up couple portrait
- ○ Wedding party portrait in (location)
- ○ Bride's family portrait in (location)
- ○ Bride with her father
- ○ Groom with his mother
- ○ Groom's family portrait in (location)
- ○ Bride, groom, and both sets of parents
- ○ Bride with her attendants
- ○ Groom with his attendants
- ○ Bride and groom with flower girl and ring bearer
- ○ Groom's attendants
- ○ Bride's attendants
- ○ Bride and maid/matron of honor
- ○ Groom and best man

Location Photography
- ○ Candid shots of wedding rehearsal
- ○ Rehearsal dinner

Pre-reception photo shoot location
After the ceremony and prior to the reception, many couples often elect to have their photos taken at a nearby garden, park, or other location that makes a striking photo backdrop

On the day of the wedding
- ○ The bride dressing
- ○ The groom dressing
- ○ The bride with her parents before leaving for the ceremony
- ○ The wedding gown
- ○ The bride's shoes
- ○ Special accessories (an heirloom necklace or earrings)

At the ceremony site
- ○ The ceremony site exterior
- ○ The ceremony site interior
- ○ The bride's arrival at the ceremony
- ○ The groom's arrival at the ceremony
- ○ The arrival at the ceremony of specific people
- ○ The altar/chuppah/other
- ○ The processional
- ○ Specific parts of the ceremony
- ○ The recessional
- ○ The departure of the bride and groom from the ceremony site
- ○ Decor (list): _____
- ○ Other (list): _____

Reception
- ○ Wedding party arrival at reception
- ○ Couple's first dance
- ○ Reception hall set-up
- ○ Bride's dance with father
- ○ Groom's dance with mother
- ○ Bride's parents' dance
- ○ Groom's parents' dance
- ○ Cutting of the cake
- ○ The garter
- ○ Throwing the bouquet
- ○ The best man's toast
- ○ Each table (guests)
- ○ Candid shots of the party
- ○ Bride's bouquet
- ○ The wedding cake
- ○ Table setting

_____

_____

_____

_____

WEDDING PHOTOGRAPHY ESTIMATES (CIRCLE YOUR FINAL CHOICE)

	ESTIMATE #1	ESTIMATE #2
Photographer name/address		
Phone number		
Web site/e-mail		
Dates and times available		
Standard package description		
Standard package price		
Final files delivery date		
Special techniques		

ESTIMATE #3	ESTIMATE #4

Read your wedding photography contract carefully. Many couples are surprised to find out that their film and the right to reprint the photos remains with the photographer in many cases. Typically, the photographer will ask you to sign a photo release (or a clause in the contract will include language similar to that of a photo release), granting all rights to your image and likeness to the photographer. If you wish to buy "all rights" to your wedding-day photographs, expect to pay a higher fee.

WEDDING VIDEOGRAPHY ESTIMATES (CIRCLE YOUR FINAL CHOICE)

	ESTIMATE #1	ESTIMATE #2
Videographer name/address		
Phone number		
Web site/e-mail		
Dates and times available		
Standard package description		
Standard package price		
Special techniques & equipment		
Extras (rehearsal dinner, shower, after party, other)		
Final delivery format		
Final file delivery date		

ESTIMATE #3	ESTIMATE #4

Ten Months Ahead

TASKS:

○ Create your personal improvement plan

○ Assemble your experts

○ Register for gifts

TOOLS:

○ Expert Resource Worksheet

○ Medical Checkup Worksheet

○ Registry Chart

Create Your Personal Improvement Plan

Many brides and grooms worry about how they will look on their wedding day. It's only natural that you both want to look and feel as good as you can on your special day. Looking and feeling your best can take some effort and planning. After all, the months leading up to your wedding will be incredibly busy, and stress and lack of time are two of the most common reasons why people don't take care of themselves.

The secret to looking fabulous on your wedding day is to utilize the same skills you do in other areas of your life — business, school, career, sports, and even wedding planning — in the beauty arena. And you can embark on this enhancement program together, because these days, men are just as prone to grooming and taking care of their overall appearance as women. You need to do the following:

- Assess your situation
- Set goals and priorities
- Assemble helpful resources
- Create a plan
- Associate the plan with a timeline
- Commit to following your plan

HEALTHY EATING

Research shows that at any given moment, a majority of American women and men wish that they could become both slimmer and more fit. When you are months away from your wedding — the day you want to look better than ever — the desire to lose weight can become even stronger, especially if the stress of planning this important event has caused you to gain a few pounds in the first place.

Programs that help people shed pounds, sensibly recommend losing weight slowly through lifestyle changes. Even if you have no weight to lose, eating healthfully provides you with the proper food and nutrition to deal with the pressure that planning a wedding adds to your already busy days.

Before embarking on any healthy eating program, know that extreme dieting and rapid weight loss can lead to gallstones, constipation, muscle cramps, and a host of other ills. Dieting can also exacerbate existing medical problems. That's why it's important to check with your doctor before changing your diet, and to ask assistance from a nutritionist before creating your meal plan. Caloric needs are different for different people, so, again, recruit an expert to help tailor a program for you.

Assemble Your Experts

Don't wait until days before your wedding to figure out your final look. Depending on your personal goals, you may need to assemble some experts — some for now and some for later — to help you achieve your overall plan. While assembling your team, it helps to clip pictures from magazines or save digital images that represent the look or image you'd like to present, so everyone is on the same page. That way you will run less risk of telling a hairstylist or makeup person one thing and discovering to your dismay that the person interpreted what you said completely differently.

Many salons and spas offer special packages targeted toward the bride and groom. They typically include a pre-wedding consultation (bring your headpiece), and then the couple returns on or before the wedding day for a massage, manicure, pedicure, shave, hairstyling with headpiece, and wedding makeup application. Some salons or personal image consultants will perform these services at your home for an extra fee.

Salons and spas also offer days of beauty onsite, perfect for bridesmaids' parties or a special pre-wedding mom and daughter day. Be sure to ask about discounts for series of treatments that can be taken prior to the wedding.

Create your list of personal experts on the worksheets on pages 66-67, schedule your appointments, and enact your plan!

EXPERT RESOURCE WORKSHEET

	SCHEDULED APPOINTMENTS	REASON
Dermatologist Name: Address: Phone number: E-mail:		
Nutritionist Name: Address: Phone number: E-mail:		
Fitness consultant/ Trainer Name: Address: Phone number: E-mail:		
Makeup artist Name: Address: Phone number: E-mail:		
Hairstylist Name: Address: Phone number: E-mail:		
Manicurist Name: Address: Phone number: E-mail:		
Facialist/Esthetician Name: Address: Phone number: E-mail:		

	SCHEDULED APPOINTMENTS	REASON
Massage Therapist Name: Address: Phone number: E-mail:		
Course or Workshop Name: Address: Phone number: E-mail:		
Yoga Studio/Teacher Name: Address: Phone number: E-mail:		
Pilates Studio/Teacher Name: Address: Phone number: E-mail:		
Other Name: Address: Phone number: E-mail:		
Other Name: Address: Phone number: E-mail:		
Other Name: Address: Phone number: E-mail:		

As part of your overall wellness plan, get a complete medical checkup. Use this chart to set up appointments and keep track of tests and results.

	APPOINTMENTS	TESTS
General Practitioner		
Optometrist		
Dentist		
Orthodontist		
OB/GYN		
Dermatologist		
Podiatrist		
Internist		
Other		
Other		

RESULTS	FOLLOW-UPS

BEAUTY TIPS

- Start on a good skin care regime early.

- Ask for a skin analysis and a personalized skin program.

- Visit a dermatologist for any problem that needs medical attention.

- Early on, pre-wedding consultations allow time to make any changes, such as cutting or growing out your hair and your hair color, or working to improve the texture of your skin.

- Meet with makeup artists and hairstylists no later than three months in advance.

- Keep your bridal makeup natural and refined by using earthy tones. Make sure your cosmetologist has specific experience with wedding makeup and photography, so you look radiant and flawless, not washed out or overly made-up.

- Consider a variety of hairstyles. Consult with your stylist and bring in an image of your gown and your headpiece to experiment with what works best.

- An upswept hairdo or a style that pulls hair back from the face in a twisted or loose bun exposes the neck, shows the gown, and forms a feminine, classic line. Your face also will be visible in your wedding pictures.

- Let your eyebrows grow out, then begin a waxing regimen for optimum shape.

- Consult with your dentist about teeth whitening and straightening options.

- If tanning is a must for your wedding, see an airbrush specialist rather than a tanning salon that uses UV equipment.

Register for Gifts

It may seem early to register for wedding gifts, but friends and family will start giving you gifts at pre-wedding gatherings such as the bridal shower and engagement party, so it's important to set this process in motion early in your planning.

Registering for gifts is a time-honored tradition, yet some couples feel a bit funny about registering. If you don't register, chances are you will receive either duplicates of items or items that do not suit your needs or style. Returning said items can turn into a terrible headache, particularly with out-of-town guests. Of course, if you and your partner are more established, or you have been married before, you may feel uncomfortable about registering. One way to get around this is by asking people to donate money to a charity in the name of a deceased parent, friend, or relative, or for a particular cause that is near and dear to your hearts. Another option is to register for experiences such as theater tickets, hot air balloon rides, dining out, and even honeymoon expenses. Registering for funds is getting easier every day through established wedding Web sites.

Most chain stores, including specialty stores, as well as furniture stores, houseware stores, travel agencies, and a myriad of online businesses, offer a bridal or wedding gift registry. Registering in-store and online are both easy to do, so talk about your needs and wishes, and get some sort of registry started now. When registering, be considerate of your guests' varied financial situations and choose a variety of items in different price ranges, so everyone will be able to find something that's in line with what they want to spend. Once you're registered, count on a friend or relative to convey the whereabouts of your list to appropriate parties, and don't forget to add the information (and links if applicable) to your personal wedding Web site.

REGISTRY CHART

Before you register, you may wish to do some research on designs and manufacturers. For example, as you visit stores or online sites, jot down the names of several china patterns that catch your eye. If a couple of people tell you what their favorite blender is, record the brand names below. Then, when you do register, you will have a good idea in advance about which items will suit your needs best, last the longest, and offer the best value.

CATEGORY	MODEL/PATTERN NUMBER	DESCRIPTION	PRICING/BENEFITS
Kitchen			
Bathroom			

CATEGORY	MODEL/PATTERN NUMBER	DESCRIPTION	PRICING/BENEFITS
Bedroom			
Yard/landscape			
Other			

Nine Months Ahead

TASKS:

- ◯ Choose your wedding theme and decor
- ◯ Select music and entertainment

TOOLS:

- ◯ Decor Supplier Worksheet
- ◯ Music Budget Worksheet
- ◯ Music Quote Worksheet

Choose Your Wedding Theme and Decor

You've always imagined your wedding would be special and unique. Yet, everyone you talk to — from the caterer to the officiant — seems to be handing you a script. The reception hall gives you a four- or five-hour package with a start and end time. The clergyperson hands you a ceremony from which you cannot deviate. The bandleader has a standard playlist. What are your options?

There are plenty of ways you can give your wedding celebration a distinctive ambience, one that reflects the personalities of both the bride and groom. Refer back to your dream wedding board (or folder of ideas) to see if there are any elements you can recreate for your wedding. Here are some ways to approach your theme and decor:

Choose a theme: Whether you want a traditional wedding or one that is unconventional, deciding on a theme for your wedding helps you to save time by focusing your attention on specific goals. This allows you to set priorities and skip over inappropriate suggestions or ideas. For example, if you decide upon a country-style wedding, you can immediately eliminate any decorating schemes, including colors, fabrics, flowers, and accessories, that lack that country feeling. Knowing your theme immediately opens you up to flexibility and inspiration, such as using terracotta pots filled with colorful mums to line the church aisle instead of the conventional satin ribbon and floral pew markers.

Choose a palette: Putting a wedding together involves a lot of interior design. Think like a good interior designer, and select a color palette. Choose one main color that is either warm or cool, and a secondary, "accent" color that is the opposite of the first. Warm colors are red, pink, and yellow. Cool colors are blue, green, and sometimes purple. Contrast a warm color with a cool color or imagine a single color such as white on white, a butter yellow, or a pale pink. Textures, shape, and weight all play a part in everything from the gown to invitations, flowers, table designs, and even food.

Accessorize: Creative table accents go a long way toward giving your wedding a one-of-a-kind ambience. For example, if one of you is interested in trains, why not work them into the centerpiece? How about placing picture frames of

the two of you as children or during your courtship, on each table? If you're having a beach-themed wedding, place pretty lanterns, shells, or beach glass around the centerpieces. Rent chair covers and beautiful table linens to add a custom flair to the decor. Let your imagination guide you.

Feature creative entertainment or entertainers: Spice up the party by including unexpected games or activities that will charm your guests. If you and your intended enjoy golf, arrange for time at the putting green during cocktails.

Other ideas: Have a hula hoop contest. Rent a photo booth or cotton candy machines for guests to have fun with. Stage a karaoke contest. Ask your bridal party to create in advance a photo montage, or a spirited PowerPoint presentation featuring the two of you, and then run it on a large overhead screen during the reception. Live video footage of the reception can also be transmitted onto a screen, as it happens. Surprise guests with humorous toasts, poems, or speeches aimed at various family members or friends.

Appreciate your guests with thoughtful gestures: If the ladies room at your catering hall is less than luxurious, consider decorating the counter with a beautiful piece of fabric and a gift basket stocked with sample soaps, beauty aids, and lotions. Or send everyone off with a bag of breakfast treats (bagels, Danish) for the following morning's consumption. This will make your guests feel appreciated, and make your wedding one they'll remember!

Go global: If you and your groom come from different cultural backgrounds, offer stations serving your special cuisine during the cocktail hour. Ethnic music can accompany the festivities, as well.

Go local: Serve locally or regionally sourced food and drink at your reception and provide an annotated menu highlighting the farms, venues, and nearby sources for the meal. Decorate with local wildflowers or natural elements from around the region. Look for locally made items to give as favors.

Plan for Special Decor

Now that you have chosen a theme for your wedding and thought of ideas to make it unique, this is the time to be in touch with vendors about ordering those special touches. Or, if you're the DIY type, make a plan for getting your supplies and a schedule for crafting the special items you've decided to include. Ordering decor items can include everything from renting tables and chairs to candelabra and outdoor tent heaters. Use the worksheet on the opposite page to track suppliers, costs, and more.

DECOR SUPPLIER WORKSHEET

Supplier Name:		Phone no:	
Address:		E-mail:	
		Web site:	

Item:	Description:	Cost:	Order Date:	Deposit:	Balance Due:

Supplier Name:		Phone no:	
Address:		E-mail:	
		Web site:	

Item:	Description:	Cost:	Order Date:	Deposit:	Balance Due:

Supplier Name:		Phone no:	
Address:		E-mail:	
		Web site:	

Item:	Description:	Cost:	Order Date:	Deposit:	Balance Due:

Select Your Music and Entertainment

Take some time to consider how music can create atmosphere and highlight the most meaningful aspects of your special day. Although most couples equate wedding music to a band or DJ for the reception, there are many other opportunities to incorporate music into your wedding. By doing so, you announce to guests that your event is truly special and something much more than an ordinary party.

Well-orchestrated wedding music is akin to the soundtrack of a good movie, framing your special occasion, signaling its beginning, middle, and end, and drawing attention to its most significant moments. A traditional scenario is to book classical or liturgical music for the ceremony; a solo pianist, harpist, folk group or ethnic performer for the cocktail hour; and a dance band or DJ for the dinner itself.

During traditional weddings, incidental music is played as guests arrive. The walk down the aisle is almost always accompanied by ceremonial music paced to dramatize the importance of the wedding procession. A fanfare of music trumpeted by a brass quintet, a triumphant march performed by the church organist, or ethnic music, such as a bagpiper or harpist for those who wish to celebrate their Celtic roots, are among the most popular choices for

CHECK YOUR VENUE'S RULES

Religious custom dictates what music is allowed in churches, so, if you are getting married in a place of worship, check with your officiant to see if there are any restrictions on what can and cannot be played during your ceremony. For example, even though many people of Irish heritage are Catholic, Catholic churches often won't allow "pagan" Celtic music, even when this is not an officially published policy. Some synagogues will allow only certain Klezmer musicians to perform, based on how authentic their repertoire is. Often, churches and synagogues will require you to use house organists, vocalists, or choirs.

Of course, if your choice of venue and officiant does not tie you to tradition, you can be as creative as you like. Couples have walked down the aisle to just about every kind of music, from Broadway show tunes to Elvis Presley, from reggae to fusion.

the wedding procession. Keep in mind that couples nowadays sometimes forgo tradition, however, adding a touch of whimsy and fun to their ceremony music. The bridal party can dance down the aisle, for example, to a pop song that reflects joy and celebration. While the highlight of the ceremony itself is often accented with a solemn but joyous song rendered by a vocalist or a choir, and exit music is typically a fast-paced, celebratory instrumental or a joyous pealing of bells, couples can create their own unique musical experience here as well.

If ethnic music is not used during the ceremony, it often plays a role at the cocktail hour before the reception. This is also the time when jazz, classical, chamber music, or some other type of music difficult to dance to but favored by the couple is played. Whatever type of cocktail music you choose, however, do keep in mind that volume is important. If the music is too loud, it will disturb the process of meeting, greeting, and getting acquainted, which the cocktail hour is designed to accomplish. Cocktail music should be loud enough to set a mood and soft enough so that people can talk while it is playing.

The wedding band or DJ is the focal point of the reception music. While the ceremony and cocktail music is often booked for as little as an hour, bands and DJs typically are expected to play for longer with breaks. In the traditional wedding scenario, the purpose of the wedding band is to provide music to dance by. Since weddings are typically attended by all ages of people, it's very important that the wedding band plays a variety of music and dance pieces so no one feels left out of the party. However, a really excellent group with a more limited repertoire that almost anyone can enjoy, such as music from the big band era or rhythm and blues, is another good option. Regardless of your choice of band or DJ, it's up to you to make sure that they play the song selections that you prefer. Ask them to provide you with their master list long before the wedding. This way you can prioritize from the selection and they won't accidentally leave out your favorites. This is important if you have a special song request that might not be included in their catalog — particularly so if you and your new spouse plan a unique first dance (such as a rehearsed routine) to surprise guests with, or if the father-daughter dance will require music that is out-of-the-norm.

Often, bandleaders and DJs play the role of announcer during the reception. An experienced bandleader or DJ will have an expert sense of timing, not only for music but also for announcing the customary reception

SAVE MONEY ON THE MUSIC BY . . .

- Hiring one band/group/trio to play during the cocktail hour and for dinner and dancing — or a DJ who can spin a variety of musical styles.

- Book a local band or DJ, so you don't have to pay transportation and/or lodging expenses.

- Have a non-continuous contract (one where the musicians break every hour) or have them play after dinner for fewer hours.

- Plan an informal wedding for which a smaller musical group is appropriate, for example, a wedding breakfast, tea, or cocktail reception.

- Create your own playlist on an electronic device such as an iPod, for background music during the cocktail hour. Just be certain that it can be connected to a speaker system.

highlights, such as the bride and groom's first dance together, the toast, the cutting of the cake, and so on.

If you are not musically inclined, ask the musicians for suggestions. Professional musicians can choose from huge repertoires, sight-read from music sheets, or, with plenty of advance notice, can learn the music of your choice.

TIPS FOR CHOOSING A MUSICAL GROUP

- Ask if the musician is planning a showcase where you can listen to a performance.

- Ask for a free demo CD or find out if they showcase their performances on their Web site.

- Make sure that the musicians you hear are the ones that will be performing.

- Ask about the possibility of last-minute substitutions.

- Verify the length of time the band will play and the frequency and number of breaks for the contract price.

- Have the contract specify whether the band will be able to play longer if you change your mind at the last minute, or whether they will have to leave for another reception. If they can play longer, expect to pay an additional hourly rate. Make sure that's included in the contract.

- Book six to eight months in advance; many good musicians are booked a year or more ahead.

- Expect to make a deposit when you book the musician and sign the contract.

- Ensure the contract specifies that a part of your deposit money will be returned to you if you cancel for any reason.

- Ask if the band carries insurance, and if so, what its coverage and liability is.

- If the band is not local, verify whether you will be expected to pay for transportation and lodging fees.

MUSIC BUDGET WORKSHEET

Use the worksheet below to brainstorm your ideas and jot down a ballpark estimate of how you will divide your entertainment dollars.

EVENT	TYPE OF ACT	ESTIMATED COST	NOTES
Rehearsal Dinner			
Ceremony			
Cocktail Party			
Reception			
Other (Engagement party, bridesmaids' lunch, post-wedding party)			

MUSIC QUOTE WORKSHEET (CIRCLE YOUR FINAL CHOICE)

This worksheet contains the questions that are important to consider as you talk with any singer, band, DJ, or other entertainer whom you are considering booking for your wedding. To help prevent misunderstandings, it's important to keep accurate notes as you interview. Once you've collected this information, you will be able to come up with a couple of possible entertainment scenarios. Then,

	ESTIMATE #1	ESTIMATE #2
Type of event (indicate Ceremony, Reception, etc.,)		
Name of band/musician/DJ/entertainer/act		
Agent or contact name, address, phone number, and e-mail		
Web site address		
Type of music played/act performed		
Number of members in group		
Length of time group has played together		
Are the performers I heard the ones likely to show up?		
Master of ceremonies?		

you can hold more detailed conversations with your preferred vendors. Ask them to send you a contract and carefully compare it to your notes to make sure it accurately reflects your verbal discussion. If you have any doubts, ask for a written clarification of the cost or service in question before signing on the dotted line.

ESTIMATE #3	ESTIMATE #4

MUSIC QUOTE WORKSHEET (CIRCLE YOUR FINAL CHOICE)

	ESTIMATE #1	ESTIMATE #2
Transportation cost		
Lodging cost		
What type of insurance does the band carry?		
Will they stay later than the contracted time period for an extra fee?		
Cost per hour to play beyond the time contracted for		
Cancellation clause		
Showcase dates and locations		
CD		
Recommended by/how I found them		
Dates and times available		
Date I requested the contract		
Comments		

ESTIMATE #3	ESTIMATE #4

Eight Months Ahead

TASKS:

- ○ Shop for your bridal gown
- ○ Order the gown and schedule fittings
- ○ Shop for wedding party attire
- ○ Choose the groom's attire

TOOLS:

- ○ Bride's Measurements
- ○ Bridal Gown Worksheet
- ○ Final Gown Choice
- ○ Bridal Attendant Measurements
- ○ Bridal Attendant Shopping Worksheet
- ○ Groom's Shopping Worksheet

Shop for Your Bridal Gown

If you're a typical bride, you probably have already been out looking for the dress of your dreams — in fact, you've probably been designing it in your thoughts off and on for decades. But choosing a wedding gown isn't all about fantasy; there are some very real issues to consider. Experienced salon professionals will say the most important question a bride should ask is whether she plans to wear the dress, or whether the dress will be wearing her.

Keeping accurate records is critical when shopping for a gown or when assembling the necessary information to place an order. The worksheets presented throughout this chapter provide plenty of room to record critical information from your shopping trips and right up to your final order.

Many women are entranced by elaborate wedding gown confectionary only to realize in retrospect that not every bridal gown style looks good on everyone. If you want to look your best, it pays to know what looks best on you and what doesn't, and choose your wedding gown accordingly. When all is said and done, the dress that's right for you is the one that looks right on you. Although there are trends in wedding gown fashion, they move much more slowly than trends in the rest of the fashion world. A popular wedding gown style may be retained in a designer's line for two or more years. Since most bridal gowns are custom-ordered, a gown that was introduced a few years ago, or one very much like it, may still be available. Additionally, wedding gowns tend to be more conservative than other clothing styles. Some wedding gown styles never go out of fashion. All of this means that you should have no trouble finding a gown that has the romantic touch you've dreamed of and the styling to show off your unique assets.

The perfect wedding dress is out there, you just have to find it. Here are some things to consider as you begin your search.

Inspiration. Begin by browsing through bridal magazines and Web sites. You're looking for qualities in the design and fabric of the dress that best express you and that will give you confidence on this magic day. Tear out or pin styles that you love and some that you simply like. Compile a solid assortment of styles. Then, visit bridal salons and boutiques (bringing the images with you) and begin trying on and comparing a variety of these gowns; you'll discover what suits you the best.

Take your theme into account. Imagine a bride wearing a glittery, poufy, Cinderella ball gown at an afternoon backyard wedding reception. You'd probably think the dress was over-the-top, too fancy, and completely wrong for such an informal affair. And you'd be right. Your gown should always correspond with your wedding theme or style. A formal, black-tie wedding requires a full-length gown, for instance. If you're uncertain, consult with your wedding gown salon experts who can help you determine an appropriate style that is compatible with your theme.

CUSTOM WEDDING GOWNS

It's possible that after exhaustive shopping, you still have not found the perfect dress. Perhaps you are petite or a large-size bride-to-be. Maybe the dress you've envisioned in your mind has not been designed yet. Perhaps you've loved certain aspects of many dresses. This may be the time to consider a custom-made gown. A custom gown is created from scratch, to meet the bride's exact specifications. Every aspect — design, silhouette, fabric, construction, length, details, and embellishments — is tailor-made. Should you opt to go this route, do work with a skilled and expert seamstress, and do so several months in advance; a one-of-a-kind gown requires time and careful craftsmanship.

Consider the season. Although most reception halls have air conditioning and central heating (and with the year-round availability of winter and summer looks), you may be tempted to wear a summer gown in the winter or vice versa. But air conditioning has been known to break in the middle of a reception, and limousines have been known to get flats in the dead of winter. To be on the safe side, look for a gown that is cut in a fabric compatible with the season. For a winter wedding, consider touches of velvet with heavy fabrics such as satin, brocade, taffeta, and moiré. For a summer wedding, choose cotton, silk, linen, batiste, crepe, georgette, and organza.

What about color? Getting married in white is a relatively new tradition. As late as Victorian times, brides dressed in their best, regardless of color. True, diamond-white looks harsh against many complexions but fortunately, there is a virtual rainbow of whites and off-whites from which to choose.

FASHION ACCESSORIES

When shopping for shoes, take into account not only style, but comfort. You'll be on your feet all day and likely, most of the night. Purchase your wedding shoes long before the wedding in order to break them in (some brides and bridesmaids often end up changing into ballet flats in the middle of the wedding reception).

Adding a touch of whimsy and fun to your wedding attire can be achieved by wearing glittery flip-flops or sandals (for a beach wedding), white sneakers (outdoor, garden wedding), or boldly colored shoes — which can even be your "something blue."

A formal wedding gown can be enhanced with matching, elegant gloves. Options include full-fingered, fingerless, wrist- or elbow-length, in a number of different fabrics and designs. If you are having a winter wedding, you might opt to include a fur or velvet wrap or shrug to your ensemble. And a delicate, stylish clutch can contain day-of necessities, such as lipstick, tissues (or a lace handkerchief), and breath mints.

A growing contemporary trend shows wedding gowns with some color. Either the entire gown is a pale shade of pink, blue, or taupe, or it contains a contrasting element, such as a blue cummerbund or bow detail, silk flowers or embroidery in pastel shades, even an accent in a dramatic color such as red.

Price. Bridal gowns run all prices. Gowns by celebrity designers often command much higher prices, even if they are simply cut and have no ornamentation. It is perhaps easier to justify the cost of a gown which uses a large amount of yardage and expensive fabric, such as silk-faced satin, or elaborate detailing like hand-applied beading, embroidery, and fine European lace.

Inexpensive gowns tend to be made of synthetic materials, such as polyester chiffon, satin, or taffeta. The ornamentation may be glued on rather than sewn on by hand or machine. Seams, in some cases, may have unfinished edges.

For brides with a modest gown budget, there are options. Discount houses and even fine salons often have sample sales, where dresses might be reduced to less than half-price. Even if you find a dress that is too large or too small, a home sewer or expert tailor can rework and refashion it so it fits you perfectly. Attending designer trunk shows often provides an opportunity for a discounted price (as well as the chance to sometimes meet and work directly with the designer). Conduct online research to find gently worn wedding gowns for purchase. Also consider alternatives to the traditional wedding gown. A beautiful, white silk suit; a simple, hand-crocheted dress; or a vintage Victorian skirt and blouse would be stunning as well as easier on the budget, with the added benefit of being suitable to wear for other social occasions.

BRIDE'S MEASUREMENTS

Height:	Neck to waist:
Bust:	Waist to floor (without shoes):
Waist:	Dress size:
Hips (7" to 9" below waist):	Arm length (shoulder to wrist):
Inseam:	Upper arm circumference:
Neck:	Hat size (or circumference of head):
Across shoulders:	Shoe size:

Gown Styles

You are probably already aware of which styles, which cuts, and which dress and skirt silhouettes (basic shapes) most flatter your body (if not, read below for suggestions, and see sidebar on opposite page).

A-LINE

Narrow, fitted bodice and waist that flares slowly to a wider, floor-length hem resembling the triangular letter A; first designed by Christian Dior in the 1950s.

Best for: almost any figure; camouflages heavy bottoms.

BALLGOWN

Form-fitting, sculpted bodice descending to a fitted, natural waist, a voluminous, full skirt that billows over tulle petticoats; neckline and sleeves vary; most popular, romantic bridal silhouette since worn by Queen Victoria for her 1840 nuptials.

Best for: those with a small waist as it features a natural, fitted waistline; not good for bottom-heavy figures.

EMPIRE

High-waisted (just-below-the-bustline) gown with small, scoop-necked bodice, slim (but not body-hugging) skirt; neoclassical style immortalized by Empress Josephine, wife of Napoleon.

Best for: almost every figure; silhouette of choice for expectant brides.

MERMAID

Slender, fitted silhouette (resembling a sheath on top) that hugs the hips and thighs, then flares out at the knees; train can be mini, long, or bustled; named for the silhouette of the mythical creature of the sea.

Best for: slender figures; not advisable for bottom-heavy figures, curvaceous thighs; can be difficult to walk and sit in.

PRINCESS

Classic, regal silhouette with long, clean lines; slenderizing fabric panels and slim vertical seams extend gracefully from shoulders to the hem of long, gently flared (A-line) skirt with chapel or cathedral train; seams and darts sculpt the bodice and skirt to the body's natural lines (there is no waistline seam); neckline and sleeves vary; popularized in the 1950s by Grace Kelly at her marriage to Prince Rainier of Monaco.

Best for: long, sleek lines of this style slenderize any figure or height; long vertical seams highlight or embellish the bust and hips, minimize the waistline.

SHEATH

Narrow, form-fitting bodice and skirt, no waistline; seams and darts flatter the body's natural curves; most often descends ankle length, with a slit in back, front, or on the side — to facilitate walking; classic style popularized by Marilyn Monroe in the 1950s.

Best for: evenly proportioned figures; it's a slenderizing style, not advisable for top- or bottom-heavy bodies.

A GOWN FOR EVERY BODY

Long, slender neck: consider high necklines, Victorian styling, tailored neckbands, stand-up collars

Small shoulder: consider portrait neckline, cape, leg o'mutton sleeves, cabbage rosettes on sleeves, puffed sleeves

Heavy figure: consider v-shaped neckline, elongated waist, A-line or princess-line dress, tailored suit

Large bust: consider sweetheart bodice with a curvy, heart-shape (as its name implies); the look is romantic; avoid square and off-the-shoulder necklines, asymmetrical detailing on bodice

Narrow hips: consider detailing (lace, ornamentation, horizontal banding) at bottom of skirt, empire waists, full skirts

Slim and tall: consider vintage Victorian skirt and blouse, hand-crocheted or all-over beaded dress

Broad shoulders: consider strapless gown, halter necklines, bolero jacket, asymmetrical bodice, sleeveless tailored sheath

Wedding Dress Lengths

The length of your wedding dress should be appropriate for the style of the ceremony and reception that you have planned, for the season and time of day, and for the location and site.

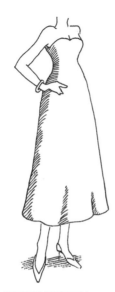

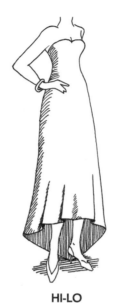

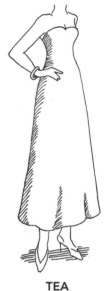

STREET

Skirt just covers the knees.

INTERMISSION

Skirt descends midway between the knee and ankle — just right for a semiformal or informal wedding.

HI-LO

Lovely combination; the hemline is intermission length in front, then descends to floor length (or even longer!) in back — elegant for a semiformal or informal wedding.

TEA

Hemline touches the bottom of the shins (about two inches above the ankles) — perfect for an afternoon garden party, a semiformal, or informal wedding.

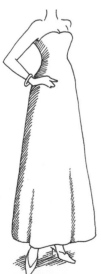

BALLET (BALLERINA)

Full, skirt swirls to right above the ankles; great bounce and verve for an outdoor celebration, a semiformal, or informal wedding.

FLOOR

Full or straight skirt gently skims the floor on all sides, a perfect choice for a semiformal wedding.

Train Styles

Most brides have a vision of the way they want to look, feel, and move in a wedding gown — it's a dream they've had their entire life! The style and length of the train that you select will have a lot to do with bringing your vision to life — as you walk down the aisle and stand with your back to your guests throughout the ceremony.

You may be interested to know that a train is a fashion detail that first appeared on gowns during the Middle Ages — a regal statement made by women at court. Back then, the longer the length, the higher the rank of the woman; today, the more yards of fabric in a train, the more formal the gown and the celebration. When choosing your train, consider the formality of your ceremony, the time of day, your site, and the length of the aisle you will walk down.

Some gowns have detachable trains, which can be easily unhooked and removed before the dancing starts. Others have no train at all, but are embellished with a bustle back — a bowed or artfully folded cascade of fabric that covers the derriere and adds flare to the back of your gown.

Another less commonly seen back detail is the Watteau train, which is attached to, and descends, from below the shoulder blades to the gown's hem. Similarly, a Watteau back features one or several wide folds (or box pleats) of fabric that flow freely from the neck, or center back, to the floor; the gown's sides and front are sashed or more closely hug the bride's figure. Both the Watteau train and Watteau back take their name from the 18th century rococo painter, Jean Antoine Watteau, whose works often featured women in similarly styled dresses.

SWEEP

The most informal and shortest train;
it barely sweeps the floor.

COURT

A short, but sweet, train; it extends just
1 foot beyond a sweep train.

CHAPEL

The most popular and more formal train; it
descends approximately 1⅓ yards from the waist.

CATHEDRAL (MONARCH)

A choice for very formal weddings; it flows
2½ yards from the waist.

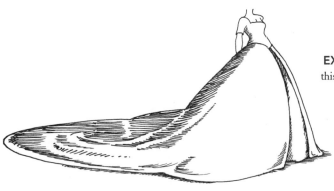

EXTENDED CATHEDRAL (ROYAL)

this most formal and majestic train cascades
at least 3 yards from the waist,
and beyond…

Neckline Styles

There is a neckline that is most flattering to every neck and bustline. Try on gowns with various neckline styles to find the perfect look just right for you.

BATEAU (BOAT)
Wide neckline that gently traces the collarbone curve; runs high in front and back and opens from one inch of each shoulder at sides, ending in shoulder seams; shows less décolletage; can be matched with sleeveless dress, or one with sleeves.

COURT
Neckline that forms a half-square at the collar bone; higher, more modest, than a square neckline.

COWL
Soft, on-shoulder neckline that drapes, in gentle folds, from one side to the other.

HALTER
Sashlike straps wrap and fasten around the neck, featuring a low back, exposing and emphasizing shoulders and arms, creating deep armholes; best worn without a bra or with a specialty bra.

JEWEL
Round, high neckline that traces the base of the throat; enhances the bustline for small-chested brides.

OFF THE SHOULDER
Neckline gently sweeps across the chest, resting softly above the bustline, below the shoulders; highlights shoulders and collarbone; leaves shoulders exposed but covers upper arms, flattering most figures.

PORTRAIT

Off-the-shoulder neckline with an added soft, wide scoop that "frames" the shoulders, sweeping gently from side to side.

QUEEN ANNE

Regal high collar at back and sides of neck curves slowly down to a low, open, heart-shaped, bare yoke; flatters most figures.

SQUARE

Neckline that descends low, above the bustline, to form a half-square; lower than a court neckline; allows modest peek of cleavage that flatters almost every figure.

SWEETHEART

Popular neckline shaped like the upper half of a heart, found on strapless or sleeved gowns; highlights décolletage and flatters most figures.

V-NECK

V-shaped front, most flattering to medium-size busts.

WEDDING BAND

High, vertically ribbed neckline that resembles a mock turtleneck that "bands" the neck; often seen with sleeveless gowns, figure-hugging bodices; flatters chest area.

Wedding Veils

Most veils are made from bridal illusion — a soft silk or nylon (tulle) fabric that may be gathered on top into delicate poufs (small gathers on the crown of the headpiece), or at the back of the head in a series of horizontal loops (imagine a spread fan in ethereal white). It can have either a raw edge (left unfinished — so that the veil seems to melt away into space), or a rolled edge (the raw edge is folded a quarter-inch under, and then another quarter-inch, and then top-stitched) — so that the veil is bordered with a narrow hem.

Veils are usually a bright white (to be paired with white gowns); diamond, or off-white (best with antique white or candlelight gowns); or ivory (a match for light ivory gowns). If you discover that there will be a color difference between the hue of your white gown and the veil, always choose a veil that is a shade lighter (not darker) than your gown.

Does your gown have a lovely back bustle or bow, or tiny buttons that trail down the back bodice? Then choose a longer veil; although sheer, tulle is much more transparent when cut in a long swath. Also realize that where you position the veil on your head affects where the veil will fall (i.e., if you position it near the back of your head, the veil will be longer).

The perfect headpiece and veil will ensure an effortless, stressfree walk down the aisle. Chapel and cathedral veils can be harder to walk with and control in tight spaces. Fingertip veils are easier to manage and pair up just as elegantly with a chapel or cathedral-length train. Remember: A double-tier veil (usually two veils of varying lengths, or a veil and a blusher) is fuller and will attractively frame your face on all sides.

For an outdoor, semiformal, or informal wedding, you might opt for a simple (fresh or fabric) floral wreath; some are attached to streamers — ribbons of satin or silk that flow softly down the back and are often tied into "love knots."

With a street-length dress or suit, perhaps choose a small, close-fitting, brimless hat (such as a pillbox or toque), with attached veiling, a lace- or bead-studded headband, or consider a half-hat, covering just half the crown of the head and extending from one ear to the other. An informal garden wedding is the perfect setting to flaunt a romantic picture hat — a wide-brimmed, light-weight lace, satin, or straw chapeau, usually draped in illusion and ribbon and/or floral adornments. It may turn up to one side and become an upturned picture hat.

The illustration below shows the varied wedding veils, in descending length, starting under the chin with the elegant birdcage and the shoulder-length flyaway, then flowing to the traditional blusher, and the elbow-length, fingertip, ballet (waltz)-length, chapel, and cathedral veils.

1) Birdcage: A traditional veil (gently shirred or drawn together at the sides); reaches just below the bride's chin and is often fastened to a picture hat or pillbox hat.

2) Flyaway: Features multiple layers of illusion descending 18 inches to touch the bride's shoulders — a perfect choice for an informal wedding, an ankle-length or shorter dress.

3) Blusher: A short, single veil, about 20-24 inches long, traditionally worn over the bride's face as she walks down the aisle, then lifted back over the headpiece — when she reaches the altar or sometime during the ceremony; it may be fastened to a longer, three-tiered veil that cascades down the back of the gown or may be worn alone for a semiformal or informal ceremony.

4) Elbow: A veil that extends about 25 inches in length, to the bride's elbows; a good match for semiformal and formal weddings; shorter, trainless gowns; gowns with full skirts; brides under 5'4".

5) Fingertip: The most popular veil, which flows an ethereal 29-45 inches to the bride's fingertips, measured with arms relaxed and resting at her sides; best for semiformal and formal weddings, any gown longer than tea length, brides over 5'7".

6) Ballet: A veil that gracefully dances downward about 60 inches, reaching somewhere between the knees and ankles; best for semiformal and formal weddings.

7) Sweep: A veil that gracefully skims the floor; for formal weddings; paired with sweep train for formal weddings.

8) Chapel: A more formal veil, extending 2⅓ yards from the headpiece, or about 108 inches from the waist; best with a floor-length, long-sleeved gown; usually paired with a cathedral train or chapel train (sometimes a sweep train), for a semiformal or formal wedding.

9) Cathedral: The most elegant veil, flowing 3⅓ yards from headpiece, often cascading at least 6 inches past the train; perfect match for chapel or cathedral trains, formal and very formal weddings.

Wedding Hairstyles

The length and style of your hair are key considerations when choosing your veil and headpiece. Planning to wear your long tresses down and flowing freely around your shoulders on wedding day? A veil of any length can work with long locks, but remember that your veil should extend longer than your hair for a neat, sleek look.

If you are drawn to the longer veils — cathedral, chapel, ballet, fingertip — that cascade below your waist, remember that, because of their weight, they are worn best with sleeker hairstyles (i.e., tresses styled close to your head, with little volume on top). Discuss a chignon (a chic roll of hair at the nape of your neck) or a Juliet topknot (a tight circular twist of hair atop your head) with your hairstylist. However, if you envision your hair intricately braided and styled across the top of your head, with a regal, longer veil, ask your stylist to layer your hair over your veil, adding elegance — and stability.

The most versatile bridal hairstyle is the French twist — a low ponytail combed back into a sleek side role behind the head; wear it easily with either a long or short veil. Can't decide if you want to wear your hair up or down? Sweep your tresses up for the ceremony, then let it down for the reception. Or opt for a style that's somewhere in between — comb some of your hair back from your crown and roll it into a bun or fasten it with a spray — a loose cluster of beading, flowers, or feathers on a comb; or with a jeweled clip or barrette; or with a few well-placed hairpins with crystal tips or pearl sprays. Let the rest of your long hair flow loosely.

If you have a kicky short haircut, enjoy a flirty short veil or a few folds of pristine white tulle pinned to your crown with sparkling hairpins. Or you can be a princess for the day, wearing a glittering tiara or floral crown that tops a longer veil. Or simply slip on a glittering headband over hair of any length.

Headpiece Styles

Your headpiece and veil will truly be your crowning glory on the wedding day. Before you select yours, consider the formality of the wedding; the length, silhouette, and detailing of your gown; and the length and style of your hair. Decide if you will remove both the veil and headpiece before the reception or just the veil (it can be detachable). Try on various styles of headpieces and veils in varying lengths while wearing your dress. Or, if you can't take the dress with you when veil shopping, try on your gown and use a tape measure to determine where, on the gown, the lengths of varied bridal veils will fall. Remember, you want to highlight, not interrupt, any fashion focal points, and not compete with the silhouette or detailing of the gown. Your veil should fall below or just above where the bodice begins, not directly at the bodice — which would visually cut the gown's silhouette in half. Similarly, if your gown has a fitted waistline, the veil should fall just above, or directly below it.

FLORAL WREATH
Nymphlike circle (or garland) of greenery or flowers (fresh, silk, porcelain), often embellished with illusion and/or romantic ribbons that trail down the gown's back; worn in the middle of the forehead, across the crown, or circling a high bun.

JULIET CAP
Small, round, Renaissance-era cap that rests snugly atop the head; usually lace- or satin-covered and accented with semiprecious stones, pearls.

MANTILLA
Traditional, one-tiered, lace (or lace-trimmed illusion) head scarf, originating in Spain; usually attached to a beautifully adorned comb, it rests flat atop the hair and softly frames the face; flows downward at least waltz length.

TIARA
Regal semicircle (smaller than a half crown) of silver or gold, usually glimmering with gemstones, rhine-stones, crystals, beads, or pearls; rests crownlike atop the head; may be attached to a veil.

BRIDAL GOWN WORKSHEET

	GOWN/ITEM STYLE NUMBER/ DESIGNER	DESCRIPTION
Gown		
Headpiece		
Undergarments *(petticoat, bras, corsets)*		
Accessories *(gloves, jackets, scarves)*		
Shoes		
Other		

ALON LOCATION/CONTACT NAME/PHONE NUMBER	COST	ORDERING INFORMATION

FINAL GOWN CHOICE

	GOWN/ITEM STYLE NUMBER/ DESIGNER	DESCRIPTION	SALON LOCATION/CONTACT NAME/PHONE NUMBER
Gown			
Headpiece			
Undergarments *(petticoat, bras, corsets)*			
Accessories *(gloves, jackets, scarves)*			
Shoes			
Other			

COST	DEPOSIT/DATE	BALANCE DUE	ARRIVAL DATE	FITTING DATE	PICK-UP

Order the Gown

Most salons require a deposit of 50% of the cost of your gown at the time you order it and the balance at the first fitting. Alterations are an additional expense. Almost all bridal gowns require some kind of alteration. Ask if the salon has an in-house tailor to fit the gown to your body and inquire about the cost. Read all contracts carefully and order well in advance of your wedding to allow for problems in delivery, fitting, and alterations.

Shop for Wedding Party Attire

You can utilize much of the previous information when shopping for attendants' dresses. Most brides want their bridesmaids to wear dresses that reflect the same styling as their own. Dressing so many different figures in the same outfit can be a problem, though. You might wish to opt for several different dress styles all made in the same color and material.

It is a traditional joke in the wedding industry that most women cannot wear their bridesmaid's dress again. Large floral prints, bright and shiny colors, and fussy detailing often distinguish bridesmaid's dresses from elegant formalwear. Be considerate of your bridesmaids when choosing a color scheme and gown style. Today, it is not unusual for bridesmaids to glide down the aisle garbed in a classic "little black dress." In times past, choosing a cocktail dress for a bridesmaid's dress would have been considered shocking; today many consider it praiseworthy.

Contemporary cocktail dresses come in a large assortment of styles and colors, and from mini- to knee- to tea-length. The flexible, modern bride often allows her bridesmaids to alter their dress's neckline or hemline to suit each one's personal taste and shape.

BRIDAL ATTENDANT SHOPPING WORKSHEET

	GOWN/ITEM STYLE NUMBER/ DESIGNER	DESCRIPTION	SALON LOCATION/CONTACT NAME/PHONE NUMBER
Gown			
Headpiece			
Undergarments (petticoat, bras, corsets)			
Accessories (gloves, jackets, scarves)			
Shoes			
Other			

BRIDAL ATTENDANT CONTACT INFORMATION

Name:	
Address:	
Phone no:	
Bridal Party Member:	
Coloring/other features:	

COST	DEPOSIT/DATE	BALANCE DUE	ARRIVAL DATE	FITTING DATE	PICK-UP

BRIDAL ATTENDANT MEASUREMENTS

Height:	Neck to waist:
Bust:	Waist to floor *(without shoes)*:
Waist:	Dress size:
Hips *(7" to 9" below waist)*:	Arm length *(shoulder to wrist)*:
Inseam:	Upper arm circumference:
Neck:	Hat size *(or circumference of head)*:
Across shoulders:	Shoe size:

BRIDAL ATTENDANT SHOPPING WORKSHEET

	GOWN/ITEM STYLE NUMBER/ DESIGNER	DESCRIPTION	SALON LOCATION/CONTACT NAME/PHONE NUMBER
Gown			
Headpiece			
Undergarments (petticoat, bras, corsets)			
Accessories (gloves, jackets, scarves)			
Shoes			
Other			

BRIDAL ATTENDANT CONTACT INFORMATION

Name:	
Address:	
Phone no:	
Bridal Party Member:	
Coloring/other features:	

COST	DEPOSIT/DATE	BALANCE DUE	ARRIVAL DATE	FITTING DATE	PICK-UP

BRIDAL ATTENDANT MEASUREMENTS

Height:	Neck to waist:
Bust:	Waist to floor *(without shoes)*:
Waist:	Dress size:
Hips *(7" to 9" below waist)*:	Arm length *(shoulder to wrist)*:
Inseam:	Upper arm circumference:
Neck:	Hat size *(or circumference of head)*:
Across shoulders:	Shoe size:

	GOWN/ITEM STYLE NUMBER/ DESIGNER	DESCRIPTION	SALON LOCATION/CONTACT NAME/PHONE NUMBER
Gown			
Headpiece			
Undergarments (petticoat, bras, corsets)			
Accessories (gloves, jackets, scarves)			
Shoes			
Other			

BRIDAL ATTENDANT CONTACT INFORMATION

Name:	
Address:	
Phone no:	
Bridal Party Member:	
Coloring/other features:	

COST	DEPOSIT/DATE	BALANCE DUE	ARRIVAL DATE	FITTING DATE	PICK-UP

BRIDAL ATTENDANT MEASUREMENTS

Height:	Neck to waist:
Bust:	Waist to floor *(without shoes)*:
Waist:	Dress size:
Hips *(7" to 9" below waist)*:	Arm length *(shoulder to wrist)*:
Inseam:	Upper arm circumference:
Neck:	Hat size *(or circumference of head)*:
Across shoulders:	Shoe size:

BRIDAL ATTENDANT SHOPPING WORKSHEET

	GOWN/ITEM STYLE NUMBER/ DESIGNER	DESCRIPTION	SALON LOCATION/CONTACT NAME/PHONE NUMBER
Gown			
Headpiece			
Undergarments (petticoat, bras, corsets)			
Accessories (gloves, jackets, scarves)			
Shoes			
Other			

BRIDAL ATTENDANT CONTACT INFORMATION

Name:	
Address:	
Phone no:	
Bridal Party Member:	
Coloring/other features:	

COST	DEPOSIT/DATE	BALANCE DUE	ARRIVAL DATE	FITTING DATE	PICK-UP

BRIDAL ATTENDANT MEASUREMENTS

Height:	Neck to waist:
Bust:	Waist to floor *(without shoes)*:
Waist:	Dress size:
Hips *(7" to 9" below waist)*:	Arm length *(shoulder to wrist)*:
Inseam:	Upper arm circumference:
Neck:	Hat size *(or circumference of head)*:
Across shoulders:	Shoe size:

BRIDAL ATTENDANT SHOPPING WORKSHEET

	GOWN/ITEM STYLE NUMBER/ DESIGNER	DESCRIPTION	SALON LOCATION/CONTACT NAME/PHONE NUMBER
Gown			
Headpiece			
Undergarments (petticoat, bras, corsets)			
Accessories (gloves, jackets, scarves)			
Shoes			
Other			

BRIDAL ATTENDANT CONTACT INFORMATION

Name:	
Address:	
Phone no:	
Bridal Party Member:	
Coloring/other features:	

COST	DEPOSIT/DATE	BALANCE DUE	ARRIVAL DATE	FITTING DATE	PICK-UP

BRIDAL ATTENDANT MEASUREMENTS

Height:	Neck to waist:
Bust:	Waist to floor *(without shoes)*:
Waist:	Dress size:
Hips *(7" to 9" below waist)*:	Arm length *(shoulder to wrist)*:
Inseam:	Upper arm circumference:
Neck:	Hat size *(or circumference of head)*:
Across shoulders:	Shoe size:

BRIDAL ATTENDANT SHOPPING WORKSHEET

	GOWN/ITEM STYLE NUMBER/ DESIGNER	DESCRIPTION	SALON LOCATION/CONTACT NAME/PHONE NUMBER
Gown			
Headpiece			
Undergarments (petticoat, bras, corsets)			
Accessories (gloves, jackets, scarves)			
Shoes			
Other			

BRIDAL ATTENDANT CONTACT INFORMATION

Name:	
Address:	
Phone no:	
Bridal Party Member:	
Coloring/other features:	

COST	DEPOSIT/DATE	BALANCE DUE	ARRIVAL DATE	FITTING DATE	PICK-UP

BRIDAL ATTENDANT MEASUREMENTS

Height:	Neck to waist:
Bust:	Waist to floor *(without shoes)*:
Waist:	Dress size:
Hips *(7" to 9" below waist)*:	Arm length *(shoulder to wrist)*:
Inseam:	Upper arm circumference:
Neck:	Hat size *(or circumference of head)*:
Across shoulders:	Shoe size:

BRIDAL ATTENDANT SHOPPING WORKSHEET

	GOWN/ITEM STYLE NUMBER/ DESIGNER	DESCRIPTION	SALON LOCATION/CONTACT NAME/PHONE NUMBER
Gown			
Headpiece			
Undergarments (petticoat, bras, corsets)			
Accessories (gloves, jackets, scarves)			
Shoes			
Other			

BRIDAL ATTENDANT CONTACT INFORMATION

Name:	
Address:	
Phone no:	
Bridal Party Member:	
Coloring/other features:	

COST	DEPOSIT/DATE	BALANCE DUE	ARRIVAL DATE	FITTING DATE	PICK-UP

BRIDAL ATTENDANT MEASUREMENTS

Height:	Neck to waist:
Bust:	Waist to floor *(without shoes)*:
Waist:	Dress size:
Hips *(7" to 9" below waist)*:	Arm length *(shoulder to wrist)*:
Inseam:	Upper arm circumference:
Neck:	Hat size *(or circumference of head)*:
Across shoulders:	Shoe size:

BRIDAL ATTENDANT SHOPPING WORKSHEET

	GOWN/ITEM STYLE NUMBER/ DESIGNER	DESCRIPTION	SALON LOCATION/CONTACT NAME/PHONE NUMBER
Gown			
Headpiece			
Undergarments (petticoat, bras, corsets)			
Accessories (gloves, jackets, scarves)			
Shoes			
Other			

BRIDAL ATTENDANT CONTACT INFORMATION

Name:	
Address:	
Phone no:	
Bridal Party Member:	
Coloring/other features:	

OST	DEPOSIT/DATE	BALANCE DUE	ARRIVAL DATE	FITTING DATE	PICK-UP

BRIDAL ATTENDANT MEASUREMENTS

Height:	Neck to waist:
Bust:	Waist to floor *(without shoes)*:
Waist:	Dress size:
Hips *(7" to 9" below waist)*:	Arm length *(shoulder to wrist)*:
Inseam:	Upper arm circumference:
Neck:	Hat size *(or circumference of head)*:
Across shoulders:	Shoe size:

Choose the Groom's Attire

The groom's considerations in terms of attire are much the same as the bride's
— time of year, time of day, theme. Like the bride, the groom may need a
suit or tuxedo that can take him from daytime to evening with just a change
of shirt and/or tie. As you shop, use the Groom's Shopping Worksheet (see
page 132) to record pieces you both like and their cost. Although the best man
and groomsmen are responsible for taking care of their own shoes, clothing,
and accessories, you can work together to create an ensemble that not only
complements you as a couple but also the wedding party. Typically, the men's
attire does not have to be ordered as far in advance as the women's — mostly
because it is often rented or purchased off the rack — but it's smart to discuss
appropriate options for your wedding style well in advance.

Traditional Wedding Wear for Grooms and Ushers

Formal: A traditional full-dress tuxedo or tailcoat.

Morning weddings: The cutaway, also known as a morning suit, has a dark
gray coat, worn buttoned in front, which curves away gradually to tailcoat-
length in back.

Semi-formal: Tuxedos with short coats, which can be either waist- or suit-length, either single- or double-breasted.

Casual: Navy blue blazer with white shirt, red patterned tie or bow tie, and camel or gray trousers.

Colors: Black endures as the favorite color, but gray is increasingly worn for daytime, especially a deeper gray jacket paired with lighter gray pants. In summer, look for white, ivory, or silver shades. Shadow stripes and textural weaves are a contemporary trend in all colors. Traditionally, the groom's cummerbund is color-coordinated with either the satin of his lapel or the bride's gown. Ushers' cummerbunds are often matched to the color of the bridesmaids' dresses. Contemporary grooms however, forgo the cummerbund for the more modern vest, which can color-coordinate with the bridesmaids, but is more tasteful when it matches the tuxedo or suit itself (or features a pattern).

Fabrics: The most popular fabrics are still wool and silk (in weights appropriate for the season), but the trendy groom could also opt for rayon.

Shirts: A white pleated shirt with ascot or winged collar and bow tie. French cuffs add an elegant touch.

Shoes: Shiny, plain-toe tied shoes, slip-ons, or kiltie styles in black, white, or silver.

GROOMING THE GROOM

Because the wedding is no ordinary day, now is the time for the groom to take extraordinary measures with his personal appearance, beginning months ahead of time. Visit the dentist and inquire about teeth whitening. Make an appointment at a spa for several facials, spaced out ahead of the wedding day. It's also a good idea for his hair to grow out, and then to splurge on a great haircut at a modern salon (not the same old, same old barber!). While there, consider waxing eyebrows so they are well-shaped. Men these days are not shy about getting manicures and pedicures, so just before the wedding, get fingers and toes in tip-top shape, as well. As for the same old, same old barber; on the day of the wedding, have him give the groom a fabulous, professional shave. Be sure to clip stray nose and ear hair, and to touch up sideburns.

GROOM'S SHOPPING WORKSHEET

	DESIGNER/STYLE NUMBER	DESCRIPTION
Suit/Tuxedo		
Shirt		
Hat		
Accessories *(tie, tie pin, cufflinks, gloves, cummerbund, socks, suspenders)*		
Shoes		
Other		

STORE LOCATION/CONTACT NAME/PHONE NUMBER	COST	ORDERING INFORMATION

Seven Months Ahead

TASKS:

○ Make your floral choices

○ Shop for wedding cakes

○ Select sweets

○ Shop for favors

TOOLS:

○ Flower Review

○ Floral and Decor Budget Worksheet

○ Floral Bid Worksheet

○ Cake Bid Worksheet

Make Your Floral Choices

In Victorian times, brides carried bouquets of flowers chosen for their symbolic meanings. Many of those flowers, such as roses, lilies of the valley, orchids, and stephanotis, are still popular today as they express time-honored sentiments. The traditional bridal bouquet was white, however, today's bride, can choose from a wider selection of exotic flowers and colors (some natural and some artificially enhanced), offering variety and longevity.

Most flowers are available year-round, since they are imported from all over the world, including Holland, South America, and Africa. Although ordering flowers from foreign countries will not drastically increase the price, florists say that locally grown flowers are less expensive. Roses may cost more during holidays, especially Valentine's Day. Ordering flowers in season, such as tulips and hyacinths in spring, may be a frugal, appropriate choice.

Florists typically advise against some varieties of flowers. For example, lilies of the valley are very fragile and short-lived and can be very expensive to

CUTTING COSTS: FLOWERS

- If there is another wedding at the ceremony site directly before or after yours, contact the bride and discuss sharing the flowers (on pews, in aisles, at altar).
- Ask ushers to move ceremony flowers, garlands, greenery, and potted plants to the reception site — to accent the receiving line area and brighten the area leading to the ballroom.
- Select in-season flowers for your region of the country.
- Carry just one or two exquisite blooms down the aisle, instead of a tightly arranged bouquet.
- Plan an outdoor garden wedding; let nature provide the floral drama free!
- Ask your florist about borrowing/renting potted plants for your ceremony and reception sites.
- Have artistic friends of the family visit a local flower market very early on the morning of the wedding and arrange small hand-tied bouquets for bride and maids, boutonnieres, and basket centerpieces. (Note: We suggest that no one in the wedding party or immediate families of the bride and groom take on this extra responsibility!)

order, not to mention unavailable out of season. Other flowers of short duration include gardenias, anemones, and daffodils. In addition to not being long-lasting, dahlias are rarely used because they are so large.

Just as every wedding will have its own theme based on a color scheme or mood, the choice of flowers will reflect individual tastes. Although there are no hard and fast rules, combinations of different flowers can enhance the wedding's theme. For country style, try baby's breath, field daisies, gerbera daisies, heather, irises, or miniature carnations. A wildflower arrangement or bouquet consisting of bachelor's button and herbs such as sage and eucalyptus would be equally lovely. For an exotic, modern look, try calla lilies or irises. For a formal or traditional wedding, try chrysanthemums, delphiniums, freesias, gardenias, larkspur, orchids, peonies, roses, and stephanotis. For an English cottage garden feeling, try alstroemerias,

baby's breath, delphiniums, freesias, gerbera daisies, hyacinths, lilacs, lilies, sweet peas, and tulips. A green wedding might feature cultivated flowers from your region, aromatic herbs from your garden, wildflowers, and ornamental grasses; twigs and branches of evergreen plants are good for a winter wedding, as are holly, some types of heather, berries, and dried flowers.

BOUQUET SHAPES AND OPTIONS

Round: Classic simplicity, good for smaller brides, works with any wedding look, from country to Victorian.

Crescent: Structured half-moon, a more individualistic shape for a bride who wants something different.

Basket: Favorite for country or Victorian-style weddings and flower girls.

Cascade: Best for grand occasions and statuesque women who can carry it off.

Single Flower: Denotes innocence.

Wreath: An unusual shape that can evoke the country or Celtic fairy lore.

Tussy-mussy: Decorative holder popular in Victorian and Edwardian times, designed to hold flowers in a structured bouquet so the bride's gloved hand would not get soiled.

Bible with Floral Spray: An old tradition, a white bible with floral spray or large orchid attached lends a note of religiosity to the ceremony.

Biedermeier: Blooms are tightly structured in concentric circles, each circle a different colored flower.

Hand-tied: Densely packed flowers are tied together with a ribbon or wired-fabric.

Pomander: Also called a kissing ball, a ball of flowers hanging from a looped ribbon.

Nosegay: Traditionally a small, round shape inserted into a tussy-mussy or bound with ribbons and lace.

Cone: Just a few flowers are used to form a light, funnel-type of shape.

Flower Review

These handy photos will allow a quick identification of more than 50 of the most popular florals for bouquets, centerpieces, and arrangements.

Key to Flower Pricing	$ Inexpensive
	$$ Average
	$$$ Expensive

Aster, spray
Aster hybrid

COLOR: white, lavender, purple
AVAILABILITY: year-round
PRICE RANGE: $
STYLE: traditional, country, garden

Bird of paradise
Strelitzia reginae

COLOR: orange with blue
AVAILABILITY: year-round
PRICE RANGE: $$
STYLE: contemporary

Baby's breath
Gypsophila paniculata

COLOR: white
AVAILABILITY: year-round
PRICE RANGE: $
STYLE: very traditional, also country and garden, rarely in contemporary

Bouvardia hybrid

COLOR: white, pink, red
AVAILABILITY: year-round
PRICE RANGE: $$
STYLE: traditional, country, garden

Bachelor's button (cornflower)
Centaurea cyanus

COLOR: vivid blue, grows in other colors but they are not usually commercially available
AVAILABILITY: summer-fall
PRICE RANGE: $
STYLE: garden, country

Calla lily
Zantedeschia aethiopica

COLOR: standard calla lilies in white only; mini calla lilies in cream, white, yellow, orange, pink, lavender, and red
AVAILABILITY: All year
PRICE RANGE: $$ to $$$
STYLE: versatile, can be used in many styles

Billy button
Craspedia globosa

COLOR: yellow
AVAILABILITY: year-round
PRICE RANGE: $
STYLE: contemporary design

Calla lily, white
Zantedeschia aethiopica

COLOR: standard calla lilies in white only
AVAILABILITY: year-round
PRICE RANGE: $$ to $$$
STYLE: versatile, can be used in many styles

Carnation, miniature
Dianthus caryophyllus

COLOR: almost every color except blue
AVAILABILITY: year-round
PRICE RANGE: $
STYLE: traditional but can be used in almost any style

Dahlia
Dahlia

COLOR: white, pink, yellow, orange, lavender, purple, burgundy
AVAILABILITY: summer, limited availability at other times of the year
PRICE RANGE: $$-$$$
STYLE: versatile, fits into many styles

Chrysanthemum, Kermit pom pom
Chrysanthemum

COLOR: lime green
AVAILABILITY: year-round PRICE RANGE: $
STYLE: versatile, can be used for many styles

Daisy, Marguerite
Argyranthemum frutescens

COLOR: white, yellow, magenta, sometimes dyed other colors
AVAILABILITY: year-round
PRICE RANGE: $
STYLE: traditional, country, garden

Cymbidium

COLOR: white, pink, yellow, lavender, green, and some two-tone
AVAILABILITY: year-round
PRICE RANGE: $$$
STYLE: traditional, contemporary

Daisy mum
Chrysanthemum morifolium

COLOR: white, yellow, lavender, purple, green; many variations of type and size
AVAILABILITY: year-round
PRICE RANGE: $
STYLE: versatile, can be used in almost any style

Cymbidium orchid
Cymbidium hybrid

COLOR: white, pink, yellow, lavender, green; also some two-tone
AVAILABILITY: year-round
PRICE RANGE: $$$
STYLE: traditional, contemporary

Delphinium
Delphinium

COLOR: belladonna types: light & dark blue hybrid types: white, blue, lavender, and purple
AVAILABILITY: year-round, best in summer
PRICE RANGE: $$-$$$
STYLE: country, garden

Daffodil
Narcissus hybrid

COLOR: yellow and white; other colors in very limited availability
AVAILABILITY: winter-spring
PRICE RANGE: $
STYLE: traditional, country, garden

Freesia hybrid

COLOR: white, yellow, lavender, purple, orange, and others
AVAILABILITY: year-round
PRICE RANGE: $$
STYLE: versatile, can be used in many styles

Gardenia
Gardenia jasminoides

COLOR: white
AVAILABILITY: year-round
PRICE RANGE: $$$
STYLE: traditional bridal flower for bouquets and corsages

Iris
Iris

COLOR: blue, yellow, white, purple
AVAILABILITY: year-round
PRICE RANGE: $
STYLE: traditional, country, garden

Gay feather
Liatris

COLOR: pink, lavender, white
AVAILABILITY: summer-fall
PRICE RANGE: $$$
STYLE: country, garden

King protea
Protea cynroides

COLOR: shaded green to pink
AVAILABILITY: year-round
PRICE RANGE: $$$
STYLE: contemporary design

Gerbera
Gerbera jamesonii

COLOR: white, cream, yellow, orange, peach, red, pink; some with contrasting centers and lots of petal variations
AVAILABILITY: year-round
PRICE RANGE: $$
STYLE: versatile, can be used in many styles

Lady's mantle
Alchemilla mollis

COLOR: lime green
AVAILABILITY: late spring-summer
PRICE RANGE: $
STYLE: country, garden

Gladiolus, standard and mini *Gladiolus*

COLOR: standards: white, pink, orange, lavender, green, burgundy, purple; also some two-tone minis: white, pink
AVAILABILITY: best in summer and fall
PRICE RANGE: $
STYLE: minis versatile; standard best in contemporary

Lily, Asiatic
Lilium aziatische

COLOR: white, cream, yellow, orange, pink, red, burgundy
AVAILABILITY: year-round
PRICE RANGE: $$
STYLE: versatile, can be used in many styles

Gloriosa lily
Gloriosa rothschildiana

COLOR: two-tone red and yellow
AVAILABILITY: year-round
PRICE RANGE: $$
STYLE: contemporary design

Lily grass

COLOR: green
AVAILABILITY: year-round PRICE RANGE: $
STYLE: contemporary

Lily of the valley
Convallaria majalis

COLOR: white, also grows in pink (not commercially available)
AVAILABILITY: almost all year, limited in winter
PRICE RANGE: $$$
STYLE: traditional flower for the bride's bouquet

Matsumoto aster
Callistephus chinensis

COLOR: white, pink, purple, lavender with a yellow center
AVAILABILITY: almost year-round
PRICE RANGE: $
STYLE: traditional, country, garden

Lily, Oriental
Lilium speciosum 'Casa blanca'

COLOR: white and pink most common available colors
AVAILABILITY: year-round PRICE RANGE: $$$
STYLE: versatile, can be used in many styles

Orchid
Phalaenopsis amabilis

COLOR: white or lavender
AVAILABILITY: year-round
PRICE RANGE: $$$
STYLE: traditional

Lily, Oriental
Lilium speciosum 'Star gazer'

COLOR: white and pink most commonly available colors
AVAILABILITY: year-round
PRICE RANGE: $$$
STYLE: versatile, can be used in many styles

Peony
Paeonia officinalis

COLOR: white, all shades of pink and red; limited availability in peach and burgundy
AVAILABILITY: early summer only
PRICE RANGE: $$
STYLE: country, garden

Lisianthus, double white *Eustoma grandiflorum*

COLOR: white; also available in pink, lavender, purple, two-tone purple, white
AVAILABILITY: year-round
PRICE RANGE: $$
STYLE: versatile, can be used in many styles

Peruvian lily
Alstroemeria hybrid

COLOR: red, yellow, orange, white, pink, lavender, purple, also some bi-colors
AVAILABILITY: year-round
PRICE RANGE: $$-$$$
STYLE: versatile, can be used for many styles

Lupin (lupine)
Lupinus polyphyllus

COLOR: blue, purple, orange, red, yellow, pink, white, or a mixture of two colors
AVAILABILITY: spring-summer
PRICE RANGE: $
STYLE: country, garden

Queen Anne's lace
Ammi majus

COLOR: white
AVAILABILITY: almost all year, best in summer
PRICE RANGE: $$
STYLE: country, garden

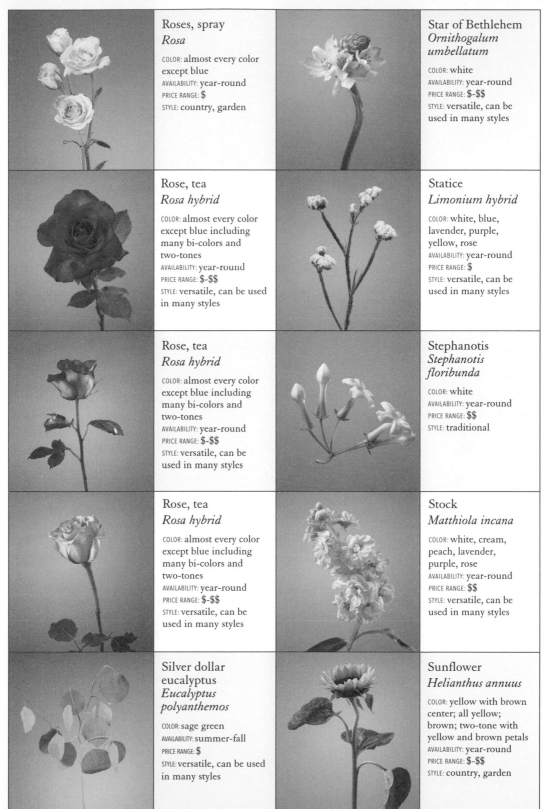

Roses, spray
Rosa

COLOR: almost every color except blue
AVAILABILITY: year-round
PRICE RANGE: $
STYLE: country, garden

Star of Bethlehem
Ornithogalum umbellatum

COLOR: white
AVAILABILITY: year-round
PRICE RANGE: $-$$
STYLE: versatile, can be used in many styles

Rose, tea
Rosa hybrid

COLOR: almost every color except blue including many bi-colors and two-tones
AVAILABILITY: year-round
PRICE RANGE: $-$$
STYLE: versatile, can be used in many styles

Statice
Limonium hybrid

COLOR: white, blue, lavender, purple, yellow, rose
AVAILABILITY: year-round
PRICE RANGE: $
STYLE: versatile, can be used in many styles

Rose, tea
Rosa hybrid

COLOR: almost every color except blue including many bi-colors and two-tones
AVAILABILITY: year-round
PRICE RANGE: $-$$
STYLE: versatile, can be used in many styles

Stephanotis
Stephanotis floribunda

COLOR: white
AVAILABILITY: year-round
PRICE RANGE: $$
STYLE: traditional

Rose, tea
Rosa hybrid

COLOR: almost every color except blue including many bi-colors and two-tones
AVAILABILITY: year-round
PRICE RANGE: $-$$
STYLE: versatile, can be used in many styles

Stock
Matthiola incana

COLOR: white, cream, peach, lavender, purple, rose
AVAILABILITY: year-round
PRICE RANGE: $$
STYLE: versatile, can be used in many styles

Silver dollar eucalyptus
Eucalyptus polyanthemos

COLOR: sage green
AVAILABILITY: summer-fall
PRICE RANGE: $
STYLE: versatile, can be used in many styles

Sunflower
Helianthus annuus

COLOR: yellow with brown center; all yellow; brown; two-tone with yellow and brown petals
AVAILABILITY: year-round
PRICE RANGE: $-$$
STYLE: country, garden

Sweet pea
Lathyrus odoratus

COLOR: white, pink, lavender, purple; other colors in limited availability
AVAILABILITY: spring-fall
PRICE RANGE: $$
STYLE: traditional, country, garden

Tulip
Tulipa hybrid

COLOR: red, white, peach, yellow, rose; all with green variation
AVAILABILITY: winter-spring; limited availability at other times
PRICE RANGE: $$
STYLE: versatile, can be used in many styles.

Sweet William
Dianthus barbatus

COLOR: vivid pink, red, purple, lavender
AVAILABILITY: summer
PRICE RANGE: $
STYLE: country, garden

Tulip
Tulip hybrid

COLOR: almost every color except green and blue
AVAILABILITY: winter-spring, limited availability at other times
PRICE RANGE: $
STYLE: versatile, can be used in many styles

Tuberose
Polianthes tuberosa

COLOR: white
AVAILABILITY: summer
PRICE RANGE: $$
STYLE: versatile, can be used in many styles

Waxflower
Chamelaucium uncinatum

COLOR: lavender or white, sometimes dyed yellow or orange in the fall
AVAILABILITY: year-round
PRICE RANGE: $
STYLE: country, garden

Tulip, parrot
Tulipa hybrid

COLOR: red, white, peach, yellow, rose; all with green variation
AVAILABILITY: winter-spring; limited availability at other times
PRICE RANGE: $$
STYLE: versatile, can be used in many styles

CEREMONY FLOWERS	TYPE	BUDGET
Runner		
Chuppah/altar flowers		
Bride's bouquet		
Bridesmaids' bouquet(s)		
Flower girl		
Bride's mother's flowers		
Groom's mother's flowers		
Groom's boutonniere		
Usher boutonnieres		
Father of the bride boutonniere		
Father of the groom boutonniere		
Other (for example, grandparents)		
RECEPTION FLOWERS		
Centerpieces		
Bride's table		
Props (columns, screens, lattice, etc.)		
Other (for example, transportation, restrooms)		

FLORAL BID WORKSHEET (CIRCLE YOUR FINAL CHOICE)

Florist Name:		Phone no:	
Address:		E-mail:	
		Web site:	

Bid#:	Approach/Style:	Cost:	Comments:

Florist Name:		Phone no:	
Address:		E-mail:	
		Web site:	

Bid#:	Approach/Style:	Cost:	Comments:

Florist Name:		Phone no:	
Address:		E-mail:	
		Web site:	

Bid#:	Approach/Style:	Cost:	Comments:

Shop for Wedding Cakes

The highlight of the wedding banquet is the wedding cake. Traditionally, it is displayed during the entire reception, and then wheeled out to the center of the dance floor on a cart. The bride and groom are invited to cut the cake, and they feed each other a small piece. Then the cake is whisked away behind the scenes, to be cut up into individual pieces that are brought to the guests seated at their tables. Pieces of wedding cake are sometimes boxed for guests to take home and slip under their pillows to inspire dreams of love and romance. Traditionally, the top layer of the cake is removed and saved for the couple to enjoy at their first anniversary celebration.

The earliest wedding cakes were piles of buns presented as offerings to ensure a bride's fertility. The traditional wedding cake, however, with its tiers festooned with butter cream swags, dates back to the court of Marie Antoinette. The royal pastry chef, Karame, longed to be an architect, but ended up as a cook. He used his passion for architecture to create elaborate castles and palaces of sugar, and the traditional modern wedding cake was born.

Today there are many cake artists who can create equally magnificent creations in flour and sugar. However, many of these are freelance cake "couturiers" that operate away from corner bakeries. If you are interested in something special, perhaps a shape associated with an interest you both share, these days wedding cake masters can be found in virtually every town. In addition, some bakeries can ship custom-made wedding cakes across the country.

Do-it-yourselfers can find materials for creating fancy cakes, including molds and plastic architectural embellishments, such as sweeping staircases and gazebos, at any major arts-and-crafts store. Of course, if you do take on this responsibility, make sure you have the time and skills required to present a beautiful and tasty product at your reception.

A CAKE FOR ALL REASONS

It's a lovely gesture to offer cake at other wedding-related celebrations, such as the rehearsal dinner (where a groom's cake is often presented) and the bridal shower. Other alternatives to an actual cake include cupcake towers, doughnut towers, whoopie pie towers, cookie cakes, or an assortment of freshly baked pies.

Cake Flavors

Traditionally, weddings have one cake for the bride (the wedding cake) and one for the groom. The traditional wedding cake comes in three basic flavors: white, yellow pound, or fruitcake, while the groom's cake was a fruitcake. Today's palates are more sophisticated, and many couples opt for chocolate, carrot, red velvet cakes, or just about any other flavor that makes them feel good. Fruit fillings, such as raspberry or apricot jam, applied between cake layers, also are popular.

Cake Decorations

The traditional wedding cake, once covered with white icing, is now often covered instead in fondant, which is like icing but has the consistency of dough, so it's rolled out and then applied onto the cake. The result is a smooth surface that is a perfect canvas for decorating. Many contemporary couples opt for cakes today with a splash of color or completely colored. Cakes these days come in a variety of shapes and tiers, giving couples tons of options. There is no end to possible materials and methods for decorating a wedding cake. Consider this list of possibilities:

- Bas-relief work (three-dimensional decorative elements) created from sugar

- Silicone putty to make imprints of architectural features on a structure, such as moldings, which in turn can be used to make a cake mold to create these features on a cake

- Fresh floral garlands

- Assorted candies

- Icing woven in a basket-weave style

- Plastic, enhancements, such as columns, cherubs, staircases, gazebos

- Silvered confectionary beads

- Handmade porcelain-like sugar flowers, blown or pulled sugar sculptures or balls

CAKE BID WORKSHEET (CIRCLE YOUR FINAL CHOICE)

Bakery Name:		Phone no:	
Address:		E-mail:	
		Web site:	

Style	Size	Cake type	Filling	Frosting	Decoration	Cost	Order date	Deposit	Balance due

Bakery Name:		Phone no:	
Address:		E-mail:	
		Web site:	

Style	Size	Cake type	Filling	Frosting	Decoration	Cost	Order date	Deposit	Balance due

Bakery Name:		Phone no:	
Address:		E-mail:	
		Web site:	

Style	Size	Cake type	Filling	Frosting	Decoration	Cost	Order date	Deposit	Balance due

Select Sweets: The Viennese Table

A Viennese pastry table is the perfect conclusion to an elegant wedding. Just as the party starts to wind down, and guests brace themselves for departure, out comes the culinary grand finale: a tiered banquet table, upon which is displayed a vast selection of pastries, confections, fresh fruits, mousses, and creams served with coffee and liqueurs. Divine!

More than just a dessert buffet, the Viennese table is a complete course in itself. Offered either in place of a served dessert, or as an added course before the end of the reception, the Viennese table presents a grand selection of pastries and confections served with fresh fruits, mousses, creams, and liqueurs.

Guests choose their sweets from a table stylishly decorated with flowers, candles, or ice sculptures. Used as a dessert buffet, the Viennese table acts to bring back the party atmosphere after a filling dinner.

Sometimes served after the closing of the bar, the Viennese table also provides the added benefit of allowing guests who have been drinking to prepare for the drive home.

While almost any kind of sweet can be used, most Viennese tables consist of a number of mini-pastries popular in Austria. Miniature éclairs, napoleons, and assorted miniature cream puffs are favorites. Classic tortes — cakes rich with eggs, butter, and a variety of fillings in which ground nuts take the place of flour — are mainstays. The jam-filled linzer and chocolate Sacher tortes often top the list. Fresh fruit, flavored mousses, and fruit tarts are also very popular, and cordials and an international coffee bar are often included. As additions, crepes, desserts flambé, or fondues are also available through some caterers. Coffees and cordials or liqueurs (often served in miniature chocolate cups) accompany this sugar spectacular.

In addition to sugar, the unifying theme of the presentation is miniaturization, so guests can sample an array of sweet tidbits.

Grand though the traditional pastry table is in itself, some contemporary caterers feel they have to add a unique, theatrical edge to the final moment, and so more extreme additions to the presentation of this course are occasionally offered, such as dancing waiters with sparklers.

While some caterers offer prearranged packages that include a Viennese table with the reception, many others will create a custom selection based on the couple's preference and charge an additional Viennese table fee per guest, on top of the package price for the wedding reception. Be sure to inquire about sugar-free, gluten-free, or vegan options if you are expecting guests with those special dietary needs.

OTHER DESSERT OPTIONS

Small-scale, informal, and even some contemporary weddings forgo the Viennese table altogether, instead opting for a creative alternative. Some couples prefer to serve passed desserts — a variety of bite-sized individual desserts offered by the waitstaff to guests while they sit at their tables or to those on the dance floor. Other couples may wish to stick with a dessert banquet table, but change up the theme. If you are an ice cream fanatic, consider a sundae bar with lots of fun fixings. A fancy coffee cart may be all you need to wrap up your festivities. Prefer candy over pastries? A brightly colored candy bar with glass jars full of your favorite varieties and scoops and to-go bags are a fun option. If you or your fiancé are more of a cookie monster type, you might consider a grand cookie bar featuring selections from your favorite bakery, or even the baking skills of friends and family if they wish to be involved. If you've already maxed out your catering budget or the traditional Viennese Table is just not right for you, this additional "course" is a perfect time to get creative.

Shop for Favors

The modern wedding often includes the tradition of giving each guest a wedding memento usually engraved, stamped, or printed with the couple's name and the wedding date. Some crafty couples opt to create their own favors. With a plethora of options now available online, couples have become ever-more inventive in purchasing or making favors that reflect their personal interests or wedding theme.

From gift packs featuring specialty local goods to small potted herbs or succulents (you can decorate the pots) to custom-made novelty items that showcase your personalities, the possibilities are endless. A growing and gracious trend in wedding favors is for couples to skip the traditional guest gift and instead donate money to a favored charity or cause. A tasteful card or note is then placed on each guest's place setting, announcing which charity was gifted in their honor to commemorate the blessings of the day.

Because this is a fairly quiet time in the wedding planning process, it's the perfect time to dive into shopping for or making guest favors. If you're planning on making something, don't leave the project until the last minute. What might sound like a fun project now will likely become stressful if you leave it until the final month before your wedding.

Six Months Ahead

TASKS:

○ Finalize the guest list
○ Plan wedding party events
○ Plan the toasts

TOOLS:

○ Guest List Organizer
○ Sample Wedding Toasts

Finalize the Guest List

Deciding whom to invite to your wedding often takes a lot of diplomacy. There are friends, relatives, and sometimes, even business acquaintances to consider when preparing your initial guest list. Now that it's time to finalize the general list you created earlier, perhaps you find yourself in the unfortunate position of being caught in the middle of a parent's divorce or having to deal with unpleasant family politics. (It can happen in the best families.) Money is often a consideration. You may not have the budget to invite everyone, and, even if you do, inviting the whole office may seem a bit over-the-top if you truly are not close to everyone.

In the case of divorced parents and steps, sometimes a wedding stirs up old sensitivities and unresolved resentments, which could place you and your fiancé in the middle of these issues. You can try to avoid this simply by choosing not to take sides and by not engaging in emotional warfare. If problems do seem to get out of control, seek counseling from a professional or guidance from a trusted friend or relative.

One common question that tends to arise when the final guest list is compiled is that of inviting children. If you plan on having children participate in the ceremony, then clearly they are special enough to you to attend the reception. Depending on their ages, you may want to hire entertainment to keep them amused and active during this otherwise adult affair. A clown, magician, or even a babysitter would fit the bill. As for inviting children who are not part of the ceremony, it's entirely up to you. Ask yourselves this: Do you feel close to the whole family? Can you identify if the kids can handle an all-day (or evening) event? Would the children enjoy themselves? Is your wedding child-friendly? Will there be an appealing menu and a table specifically for kids?

Here's what not to ask yourselves: Will the parents be offended if their children are not invited?

Keep in mind the old adage — you can't please everyone all the time. This is particularly true when it comes to your wedding guest list, so do what will make you both happy and fulfilled and at ease with your decisions.

In days past, etiquette spelled out who threw which of these events, and who was permitted to attend. Back then, for example, the parents threw the engagement party, the bride never attended the stag party, and so on. Today, however, many of these traditional boundaries have been somewhat diminished. Some brides throw their own bridal showers, while others have no qualms about attending the bachelor party. A number of contemporary couples opt for Jack and Jill showers, which are attended by both male and female guests. After-parties, held immediately after the reception either at the same site or at a dance club or bar, are gaining in popularity. Is all of this proper? That depends on the circles you travel in, how individualistic and modern you are, and the nuances of what passes for acceptable behavior in your own select circle of friends.

You may decide to skip some of the customary parties associated with a wedding. That's fine. But, for those who are preparing a wedding with

traditional fanfare, we've provided columns on the worksheet for the most common parties held during the yearlong wedding-planning process. A majority of the parties are held later in the planning, only one, the engagement party, is celebrated early on. Enter a check in the box if you expect to invite that person to one of those events or if someone else throws a party in your honor and invites that person. Even if you do not do the inviting and preparation for that specific party, it helps to keep track of who attended. Naturally you will want to thank them for attending any event held in your honor and for any gift they might give you. You also can cross-reference your parties to ensure that you do not overlook anyone who attended one party when you are compiling guest lists for another party.

On the Guest List Organizer, the day of the big event is color-coded. In these columns, you can indicate whether the person was invited to the reception and ceremony or the ceremony only, and whether they have accepted or regretted your invitations.

GUEST LIST ORGANIZER

Guest #	NAME	RELATIONSHIP (GROOM, BRIDE OR OTHER)	ADDRESS, TELEPHONE, E-MAIL
1			
2			
3			
4			
5			
6			
7			
8			
9			
10			
11			
12			
13			
14			
15			
16			
17			
18			
19			
20			
21			
22			
23			
24			
25			

ENGAGEMENT PARTY	BRIDESMAID'S LUNCH	BRIDAL SHOWER	GROOM'S OUTING	OUT-OF-TOWN GUESTS	BACHELOR BACHELORETTE PARTY	REHEARSAL DINNER	CEREMONY	RECEPTION			AFTER PARTY	AFTER-RECEPTION BRUNCH	OPEN HOUSE
EP	BL	BS	GO	OTG	B/BP	RD	C	R	ACCEPT	REGRET	AP	ARB	OH

GUEST LIST ORGANIZER

Guest #	NAME	RELATIONSHIP (GROOM, BRIDE OR OTHER)	ADDRESS, TELEPHONE, E-MAIL
26			
27			
28			
29			
30			
31			
32			
33			
34			
35			
36			
37			
38			
39			
40			
41			
42			
43			
44			
45			
46			
47			
48			
49			
50			

ENGAGEMENT PARTY	BRIDESMAID'S LUNCH	BRIDAL SHOWER	GROOM'S OUTING	OUT-OF-TOWN GUESTS	BACHELOR BACHELORETTE PARTY	REHEARSAL DINNER	CEREMONY	RECEPTION			AFTER PARTY	AFTER-RECEPTION BRUNCH	OPEN HOUSE
EP	BL	BS	GO	OTG	B/BP	RD	C	R	ACCEPT	REGRET	AP	ARB	OH

Guest #	NAME	RELATIONSHIP (GROOM, BRIDE OR OTHER)	ADDRESS, TELEPHONE, E-MAIL
51			
52			
53			
54			
55			
56			
57			
58			
59			
60			
61			
62			
63			
64			
65			
66			
67			
68			
69			
70			
71			
72			
73			
74			
75			

ENGAGEMENT PARTY	BRIDESMAID'S LUNCH	BRIDAL SHOWER	GROOM'S OUTING	OUT-OF-TOWN GUESTS	BACHELOR BACHELORETTE PARTY	REHEARSAL DINNER	CEREMONY	RECEPTION			AFTER PARTY	AFTER-RECEPTION BRUNCH	OPEN HOUSE
EP	BL	BS	GO	OTG	B/BP	RD	C	R	ACCEPT	REGRET	AP	ARB	OH

GUEST LIST ORGANIZER

Guest #	NAME	RELATIONSHIP (GROOM, BRIDE OR OTHER)	ADDRESS, TELEPHONE, E-MAIL
76			
77			
78			
79			
80			
81			
82			
83			
84			
85			
86			
87			
88			
89			
90			
91			
92			
93			
94			
95			
96			
97			
98			
99			
100			

ENGAGEMENT PARTY	BRIDESMAID'S LUNCH	BRIDAL SHOWER	GROOM'S OUTING	OUT-OF-TOWN GUESTS	BACHELOR BACHELORETTE PARTY	REHEARSAL DINNER	CEREMONY	RECEPTION			AFTER PARTY	AFTER-RECEPTION BRUNCH	OPEN HOUSE
EP	BL	BS	GO	OTG	B/BP	RD	C	R	ACCEPT	REGRET	AP	ARB	OH

GUEST LIST ORGANIZER

Guest #	NAME	RELATIONSHIP (GROOM, BRIDE OR OTHER)	ADDRESS, TELEPHONE, E-MAIL
101			
102			
103			
104			
105			
106			
107			
108			
109			
110			
111			
112			
113			
114			
115			
116			
117			
118			
119			
120			
121			
122			
123			
124			
125			

ENGAGEMENT PARTY	BRIDESMAID'S LUNCH	BRIDAL SHOWER	GROOM'S OUTING	OUT-OF-TOWN GUESTS	BACHELOR BACHELORETTE PARTY	REHEARSAL DINNER	CEREMONY	RECEPTION			AFTER PARTY	AFTER-RECEPTION BRUNCH	OPEN HOUSE
EP	BL	BS	GO	OTG	B/BP	RD	C	R	ACCEPT	REGRET	AP	ARB	OH

GUEST LIST ORGANIZER

Guest #	NAME	RELATIONSHIP (GROOM, BRIDE OR OTHER)	ADDRESS, TELEPHONE, E-MAIL
126			
127			
128			
129			
130			
131			
132			
133			
134			
135			
136			
137			
138			
139			
140			
141			
142			
143			
144			
145			
146			
147			
148			
149			
150			

ENGAGEMENT PARTY	BRIDESMAID'S LUNCH	BRIDAL SHOWER	GROOM'S OUTING	OUT-OF-TOWN GUESTS	BACHELOR BACHELORETTE PARTY	REHEARSAL DINNER	CEREMONY	RECEPTION			AFTER PARTY	AFTER-RECEPTION BRUNCH	OPEN HOUSE
EP	BL	BS	GO	OTG	B/BP	RD	C	R	ACCEPT	REGRET	AP	ARB	OH

GUEST LIST ORGANIZER

Guest #	NAME	RELATIONSHIP (GROOM, BRIDE OR OTHER)	ADDRESS, TELEPHONE, E-MAIL
151			
152			
153			
154			
155			
156			
157			
158			
159			
160			
161			
162			
163			
164			
165			
166			
167			
168			
169			
170			
171			
172			
173			
174			
175			

| ENGAGEMENT PARTY | BRIDESMAID'S LUNCH | BRIDAL SHOWER | GROOM'S OUTING | OUT-OF-TOWN GUESTS | BACHELOR BACHELORETTE PARTY | REHEARSAL DINNER | CEREMONY | RECEPTION | ACCEPT | REGRET | AFTER PARTY | AFTER-RECEPTION BRUNCH | OPEN HOUSE |
EP	BL	BS	GO	OTG	B/BP	RD	C	R	ACCEPT	REGRET	AP	ARB	OH

Guest #	NAME	RELATIONSHIP (GROOM, BRIDE OR OTHER)	ADDRESS, TELEPHONE, E-MAIL
176			
177			
178			
179			
180			
181			
182			
183			
184			
185			
186			
187			
188			
189			
190			
191			
192			
193			
194			
195			
196			
197			
198			
199			
200			

ENGAGEMENT PARTY	BRIDESMAID'S LUNCH	BRIDAL SHOWER	GROOM'S OUTING	OUT-OF-TOWN GUESTS	BACHELOR BACHELORETTE PARTY	REHEARSAL DINNER	CEREMONY	RECEPTION	ACCEPT	REGRET	AFTER PARTY	AFTER-RECEPTION BRUNCH	OPEN HOUSE
EP	BL	BS	GO	OTG	B/BP	RD	C	R	ACCEPT	REGRET	AP	ARB	OH

Plan Wedding Party Events

The wedding day is still far away, so it may seem early to be planning a special pre-wedding thank-you party for your friends and family. But time will fly by quickly in the final days leading up to the wedding, so now is the time to make plans for a get-together.

At the party, you will probably want to thank your friends and family for all of their help with the wedding plans. You might also want to show your appreciation for their friendship over the years and spend some time reminiscing. Perhaps you'll recall summers spent together, or times when they provided you with much needed comfort or advice. Certainly, you'll want to reassure them that the relationship will continue to be important to you. Often, newly married couples go through lifestyle changes that reduce the amount of time they have available for friends. So this very personal thank-you party will be the happy occasion that they will remember with much fondness during the early days of your new marriage, when you may not be able to see them as much as you used to.

Your personal thank-you can take any number of forms. For family, perhaps a day on the golf course or sporting event. For your gal pals, consider a tea party thrown in your home or at a specialty shop, lunch at a sushi restaurant, a barbecue on the back porch, or a day at the spa (you might want to ask for a group discount). The groom and his buddies might enjoy lunch at a sports bar or a poker night. Whatever form it takes, make sure there's plenty of time to talk, laugh, and share your stories. You'll need to bank some sharing against the hectic days ahead!

Plan the Toasts

A highlight of the wedding reception is the champagne toast, proposed by the best man to the bride, first, and then to the groom, with others joining in — the maid of honor to the couple, the bride to her parents, the groom to his, and so on.

Included with many banquet hall reception fees is the cost of the champagne toast (or, more accurately, the sparkling wine toast, for many caterers typically serve champagne-like beverages that do not come directly from the Champagne region in France).

Small bottles of champagne or sparkling wine, adorned with custom labels bearing the couple's name and wedding date and perhaps a white satin bow, are popular wedding favors. Where local vineyards are plentiful, couples may gift guests with small bottles of local wine. Check with local laws; in some states (and hotels), you cannot bring cases of alcohol purchased from an outside vendor into a reception or banquet hall, and in others you can bring the small bottles in as long as they remain unstoppered or are contained in sealed bags and distributed at the end of the evening as favors.

When people think of wedding toasts, the best man and the wedding party usually come to mind. But a bride's toast to her groom and the groom celebrating his bride is a wonderful moment and they don't have to stop there. The couple can thank each other's family, their friends, the wedding party, and the guests. See page 181 for a few sample openers that may inspire you to create your own.

Traditional Toasts

The wedding reception is where the best man has a chance to shine. He is in charge of the first toast and will need to get everyone's attention as the toasts and speeches begin. The following sequence is the typical order of toasts at the wedding reception:

Best man

Groom's father

Bride's father

Groom

Bride

Friends and relatives

Maid/matron of honor

Groom's mother

Bride's mother

While some people are perfectly comfortable offering their toasts on the fly, others will want more time to prepare. Let your wedding party and family members know if you expect them to make a toast well in advance of your special day.

SAMPLE WEDDING TOASTS

TOASTS TO THE BRIDE OR GROOM BY THE SPOUSE

- *Here's to the prettiest/handsomest, here's to the wittiest,
  here's to the truest of all who are true,
  Here's to the neatest one, here's to the sweetest one,
  Here's to them, all in one — here's to you.*

- *Here's to my bride/groom: she/he knows everything about me,
  yet loves me just the same.*

- *Merry met, and merry part, I drink to thee with all my heart.*

- *(Bride), take (groom)'s hand and place his hand over yours. Now, remember this
  moment and cherish it . . . because this will be the last time you'll ever have the
  upper hand!*

- *I have known many, liked not a few, loved only one: I toast to you.*

TOASTS BY THE BRIDE OR GROOM

- *On behalf of _____ and myself, I would like to thank you all for joining us today
  as we celebrate our marriage. I know that some of you have traveled many miles
  to be here — thank you. We are honored to have you with us. As I look around
  me, I am reminded of the importance of family and friends. _____ and I are
  truly blessed in having all of you with us today to share in this joyous occasion,
  to witness our union and the coming together of our two families. Thank you all
  for your support and your love.*

The bride and groom usually thank their parents and relatives as well as the entire
wedding party including the best man and groomsmen. Finally, they thank all the guests
for attending the wedding celebration.

- **To each other:** *Family, friends, members of the wedding party, I give you_____,
  my beautiful bride/groom. I knew from the moment I saw _____ that she/he
  was my soul mate. _____, you're beautiful inside and out.*

- **To the parents of the bride:** *To _____ and _____, I thank you for
  including me in your family and for thinking of me as one of your own.*

- **To the parents of the groom:** *How can I ever thank you for all your love and
  support? You have always been there for me and I celebrate you with a toast.*

- **To the wedding guests:** *Let the celebration begin! I am honored that each of
  you is here to be part of this special day.*

- **To the best man:** *It's great to see the best man dressed for something other
  than a court appearance!*

- **To the groomsmen:** *I have shared many memories with each and everyone of
  you and I thank you for being part of this incredible day with us. It means a lot
  for you to be here.*

Five Months Ahead

TASKS:

- ○ Plan a honeymoon
- ○ Attend to legal matters
- ○ Attend to business matters

TOOLS:

- ○ Honeymoon Budget
- ○ Travel Checklist

Plan a Honeymoon

The honeymoon is a special time when couples get to know each other all over again in a new context — as husband and wife. It's also a time to relax and rejuvenate after months of wedding planning. Naturally, you want your travel plans to go as smoothly as possible, so you and your intended can focus your energies on each other. Plan now for a stress-free honeymoon by utilizing these tips and suggestions.

If you are planning a trip to another country, you may find that the date and time of your trip does not coincide with the end of your wedding reception. You will need to plan what to do during this "lag" time. Many couples book a room at an airport hotel, only to find it is one of the least romantic places to spend the wedding night, with planes taking off overhead every few minutes. To avoid this, it might be a good idea to plan to take off for your honeymoon one or two days after the wedding. The intervening time can be spent at a small bed-and-breakfast, cabin in the woods, a romantic weekend getaway, or simply holed up in your new house (decorated, cleaned, and well-stocked with gourmet nibbles ahead of time).

Some couples find that because of work schedules or other commitments, they can't go on an extended honeymoon until weeks or even months after the wedding. If that's the case, you can still have some quality, romantic time on your own by going on a local mini-moon. Research romantic areas near your hometown — perhaps a place you've never been to but have always wanted to visit, or a location that you can drive to within just a few hours. Then book a lovely hotel, small inn, or bed-and-breakfast there. When setting up your reservations, be sure to mention that you are newlyweds, as many accommodations offer special treats for recently married couples (a welcome gift of champagne and chocolate-covered strawberries, for instance). While away, pamper yourselves with spa treatments and room service. You deserve it!

If you are able to leave for your honeymoon immediately after the wedding, now is the time to discuss what type of honeymoon you would both enjoy most. This may take some negotiating skills, since it's very rare for two people to have exactly the same tastes! You may like exotic places, antiquing, and visiting museums, while your fiancé may prefer fishing and bike riding through the countryside. Many travel destinations offer a variety of experiences, and you can take advantage of this fact if you know what your priorities are and plan carefully from the start.

The type of trip you choose will also depend on how comfortable you feel traveling to unfamiliar destinations In addition, think about whether you want to plan your trip now (hotels, meals, excursions etc.,) or if you want to take it easy after all the wedding planning. If you are planning a trip to an unfamiliar place, a country where you may not speak the language, or have a tight budget, you may prefer an all-inclusive resort, tour, or cruise with a package price. This type of honeymoon offers a great convenience — everything is done for you. For instance, on a honeymoon cruise, you can expect tons of daily scheduled activities. Sometimes alcoholic beverages are prepaid, so you can dine and simply walk away without worrying about the bill.

If you already have agreed on the honeymoon destination, do a little online research to learn more about the area. Most locales have official tourism Web sites chock-full of information (and images), such as local attractions, entertainment, dining and lodging options, and upcoming events. Whatever you decide on, book it early, as that often can mean getting a discount. Also check out deals offered by airlines, travel agencies, and consumer travel Web sites.

Once you estimate the total dollar cost you plan to budget for your honeymoon, you can get down to specifics. To get a good idea of how much your dream honeymoon might cost, fill out the worksheet below.

TRANSPORTATION	
Car rental:	
Airfare:	
Train:	
Taxi:	
Tips:	
Subway:	
Airport transfers:	
Other:	
HOTEL/LODGING	
No. of nights x rate per night:	
Taxes and tips:	
Phone/fax/video fees:	
Housekeeping extras:	
Other:	
FOOD/DINING	
Number of meals per day x average cost per meal:	
Drinks:	
Gratuity:	
Other:	

ENTERTAINMENT	
Sightseeing	
Shopping	
Sports	
Theater	
Museums	
Bus fare	
Salons and spas	
Amusement parks	
Boat rides	
Beach fees	
Day excursions	
Personal sundries	
Clothes washing/laundry	
Travel insurance	
Film	
Reading matter	
Other:	
OTHER	
Petcare:	
TOTAL COST:	

TRAVEL CHECKLIST

Depending on your destination, you may need special documents and items. Consult the following checklist to be certain you have the essentials.

- ○ Airline tickets
- ○ Passport
- ○ Visas (if needed for your destination. Check http://visacentral.com)
- ○ Driver's license
- ○ Copy of birth certificate (certified)
- ○ Itinerary
- ○ Emergency phone numbers (if going abroad, check with U.S. Department of State, (www.travel.state.gov), for a list of helpful numbers to contact in case of an emergency)
- ○ Proof of inoculations (if necessary; check for government advisories on the Department of State Web site)
- ○ Names, addresses, phone numbers, and e-mail addresses of family members and relevant friends
- ○ Make 2 photocopies of credit cards, debit/electronic cash cards, and passport & visa (keep one in suitcase and leave one at home)
- ○ In case of lost luggage, a list of the contents of your luggage (each bag should be labeled inside and out, and the items on your luggage list should be organized according to each bag label) and the contact information for the lost luggage claims for the airline you are using
- ○ Credit cards
- ○ Over-the-counter medications and prescriptions, including eyeglasses
- ○ Insurance policy identity card and a claim form (be sure your health insurance provides for overseas coverage)
- ○ Tour books
- ○ Foreign phrasebook (or electronic translator)
- ○ Eurorail or other passes and tickets obtained in advance of trip
- ○ Miscellaneous travel documents
- ○ International cell phone rental plan
- ○ Electric plug adapter or converter

Attend to Legal Matters

Today a bride may choose to retain her own name or take her husband's name. Or, the couple may decide to take hyphenated names, although, for anything other than taking your husband's name or keeping your own, you will probably need to go to court to get an official order changing your name.

To take your husband's name upon marriage, first visit www.rocketlawyer. com, then start using his name consistently. A certified copy of your marriage certificate, which should be sent to you shortly after your marriage, is required to change your name on important documents such as your Social Security card. Notify government agencies and private institutions of your name change, as well as changing contracts, deeds, and stationery.

Here's a partial list of organizations, agencies, and documents affected by a name change.

- Employers
- Post office
- Department of Motor Vehicles
- Department of Records or Vital Statistics
- Banks (checking, savings, brokerage accounts, mortgage payments)
- Voter's registration
- Telephone company
- Tax offices
- Utility companies
- Powers of attorney
- Living wills

- Contracts
- Creditors or loan agencies
- Insurance companies
- Cable TV company
- Cell phone carrier
- Car title
- Business cards
- Medical records and prescriptions
- Club or organization memberships
- Retirement funds
- Investment funds
- Alumni or other associations

Attend to Business Matters

A wedding may be a romantic celebration, but amidst the joyous preparations, there are a number of business matters that should be attended to. After all, marriage is a legal union that confers both rights and responsibilities on you and your spouse. You need to consider how these will affect your lives and proceed accordingly.

At some point, either right before or shortly after marriage, you will want to consult your tax advisor, insurance expert, and attorney to discuss the ways being married will affect your legal status. Topics you should discuss include:

- Your tax returns

- Financial budgeting and planning

- Insurance policies

- Independent business ownership

- Wills

- Property owned prior to marriage

- Social Security, Medicare, and Disability benefits

- Joint checking accounts

- Trusts

- Government benefits (e.g., veteran's)

- Employment benefits (e.g., health insurance)

- Parenting and custody issues

- Legal benefits and protections provided to spouses under the law

- Premarital agreements to preserve property for children from a previous union

Four Months Ahead

TASKS:

- ○ Secure accommodations for out-of-town guests
- ○ Book wedding day transportation

Out-of-Town Guests

Guests are responsible for providing their own transportation to and from a wedding. If they live far enough away from the wedding that they need to stay overnight, they are still responsible for making reservations and paying for rooms at a nearby hotel, but there are many ways you both can help make it all easier for your out-of-town guests.

It's a nice — and welcome — gesture when the bride and groom make planning easier for guests by suggesting suitable and affordable hotels that are close to the wedding location. This can be accomplished in a relatively simple manner; check online for nearby accommodations with varying prices and e-mail or, even better, post the names, locations, and links to the places on your wedding Web site. Or, if you're inclined to go a step further, the two of you can book a block of rooms in a convenient hotel. To do this, first go over your guest list and determine how many out-of-town guests might attend the wedding. Then locate one or two suitable hotels that are near the wedding venue. Contact the sales office or the events coordinator and request their best rate to secure a block of rooms. Usually, you will not be charged for reserving a block of rooms, but they may request a deposit. The hotel will provide you with a cutoff date for your guests' reservations. After that point, they will not be guaranteed the same rate.

In many cases, if you have booked a hotel for your wedding reception, you might also receive special room discounts for wedding guests. Be sure to ask your catering establishment if such is the case, so you can pass along the information to any out-of-town guests. Even though the wedding is still months off, hotels can fill quickly, especially during popular wedding months, so inform your guests early of the lodging choices and the cut-off date for reservations.

WHO PAYS?

It's traditional for the groom or his family to pay for lodging for out-of-town groomsmen and for the bride to pay for lodging for bridesmaids who are coming from a distance. Of course, putting up wedding party members at the home of a nearby friend or relative's house is a perfectly acceptable alternative to paying pricey hotel fees.

Out-of-Town Guest Welcome Bags

Are any of your out-of-town guests unfamiliar with the area where your wedding is being held? Share what you know about the area, so they have the option of making a fun and relaxing mini-vacation out of the trip. Put together a "welcome bag" for them. You might contact your local chamber of commerce for informational brochures about exciting things to do and see in the town and surrounding area, as well as maps, and a list of car rental agencies. Because your guests will want to look their best, you can include information about beauty salons, spas, and dry-cleaning services.

You can also add personal touches, such as bottled water, gourmet chocolates, or a bottle of local wine. Not only will your guests delight in finding a lovely welcoming surprise in their rooms, you'll save them time and trouble and free them up to enjoy partying with you!

- List of local attractions
- Rental car information
- Maps
- Travel guide (check with your local chamber of commerce)
- Local newspaper or magazine

- Spas and beauty salons
- Local events
- Shopping destinations
- Dry cleaners and laundry services
- Restaurants
- Drugstores

Enclose a note with your welcome basket saying how much you appreciate the guest(s) coming such a long way to celebrate your special day with you.

Book Wedding Day Transportation

Just as with every other wedding vendor you have booked, securing reliable transportation for your wedding day is of utmost importance. That's why it's best to do it now, when the wedding is still several months away and you have time to shop around for a professional service. Typically, bride and bridesmaids are transported to the ceremony in one vehicle, and the groom and groomsmen in another A car for the parents and perhaps grandparents of the couple is also a nice gesture. Once the ceremony has taken place, the newlyweds can be whisked off to the reception either with the wedding party or in a private vehicle.

Limousines are generally rented by the hour, day, or half-day. The cost usually includes the driver, although most expect a gratuity on top of the advertised rate. Make sure the fee includes the gas. Rates are determined by size and model/make. Fancy and vintage limousines are booked early and cost the most money.

Regardless of what sort of transportation you book, be certain that you are working with a reputable firm. The contract should stipulate exactly what type of limousines you are renting (color and seating capacity) and the anticipated time of arrivals and departures from the various locations on the wedding day. If you are getting married in the spring or summer, make certain the cars will be equipped with working air-conditioning and beverages. It's also a good idea to ask about back-up plans: what happens if one of the vehicles has a flat tire on the way to the ceremony, for instance. No detail should be left up to question if you want to get to the church on time!

In addition to limousines, there are many romantic and unique ways to arrive at and depart from your wedding. Couples who are sporty have been known to bicycle their way to the reception. Perhaps renting a white horse is more suitable to you and your fiancé. Here are some other ideas:

Coaches and carriages. These include antique coaches, Victorian carriages, surreys, horse-drawn trolleys, sleighs, and carts. Drivers often dress in vintage attire. Transportation area is limited to the number of miles a horse can pull a carriage in the allotted time. Often, mileage to and from the site is included in the total.

Vintage cars. Travel in style in a vintage car with a chauffeur in a tuxedo. This is one of the classiest ways to make a grand entrance to your reception, or to leave it in high fashion. A vintage convertible is also a fun ride, but keep in mind that your hair and makeup might take a slight whipping. The average limo service will travel up to two or three hours away.

Trolleys. An old-fashioned trolley can accommodate a large group of people and is therefore perfect for transporting guests from the ceremony to the reception, provided they are not too distant from each other. Trolleys can be dressed up for the day with flowers, tulle, and other decorations.

However you opt to travel on your wedding day, discuss your plans in advance with your photographer and videographer, so that they don't miss out on any photo opportunities. And if you plan on making a splashy entrance to the reception, arrange for your guests to be outside, to witness it.

Three Months Ahead

TASKS:

- ○ Choose wedding rings
- ○ Select bridal jewelry
- ○ Mail your invitations
- ○ Learn to dance

TOOLS:

- ○ Wedding Ring Shopping Worksheet
- ○ Invitations Checklist
- ○ Dance Lessons Worksheet

Choose Your Wedding Rings

Most couples treasure the trip to the jewelry store to choose their wedding bands together. Rings are the only wedding purchases that the bride and groom will enjoy every day for years to come. As symbols of commitment, fidelity, and honor, rings are tokens most couples take the time to choose carefully.

In the traditional Western wedding, the engagement ring and the wedding band are both worn on the left ring finger, which in folklore is said to run straight to the heart.

When shopping for rings, work with a reputable jeweler. Ask for an appraisal certificate so you can insure your rings (both wedding and engagement) for the value of their replacement.

Yellow gold, once the only favored metal, has taken a back seat to platinum, which has been surging in popularity for several years. One of the rarest of all precious metals, and therefore somewhat expensive, platinum is also a hard metal that resists scratches and can last up to fifty years without showing signs of wear. Platinum jewelry also does not require any special care, but can be electro- or rhodium-plated with another precious metal, to help preserve its luster. Compared with gold, which is 58 percent pure for 14 karat, for platinum

there is a 90% pure standard, which is why many feel that, although platinum costs more, it is a better investment. Still others prefer white gold, which looks quite similar to platinum, but is less expensive.

Today, you can find a number of cutting-edge ring designs, with unique surface treatments; bold, sculptural lines; and fancy colored stone accents; as well as reproductions of antique designs from original dies in both masculine and feminine styles. There are also many craftsmen who will gladly custom-design your rings upon request. In addition, couples these days don't necessarily require matching wedding bands, so each of you can wear the ring that best suits your personal taste and lifestyle.

Wedding Bands 101

Gold has been the top choice for wedding bands for centuries and with good reason. The purity of gold is indicated by the number of karats, and 24k is about as pure as gold can be. Both 18k and 24k gold feature great color, fabulous results when mixed with other metals, and are easily shaped in molds (especially good if you are designing your own bands). Pure 24k gold is unsuitable for almost any type of jewelry, as it is too soft, but works when combined with a mixture or alloy of other metals. Choose coppor or silver if you want to retain the "gold" color. If you want "white" gold choose nickel and/or palladium (although beware of nickel as many people have allergic reactions to is so palladium might a better choice. The results are stunning and much more durable.

Eco-gold is a good choice if ethical sources of gold and even diamonds are important to you. Eco-gold is obtained either from suppliers who adhere to a strict code of ethics (fair treatment of workers and safety in the mines) or from companies who specialize in recycled jewelry or scrap.

Platinum is highly regarded for its incomparable brightness (a sensational backdrop for diamonds) and durability and, if your budget allows, is a fantastic choice.

Rhodium is another dazzler and a precious metal so it will demand a higher price, but there's really nothing like it. In jewelry, rhodium is most often used as a plating, but there is a downside to its glittering appeal: it costs more than gold and the plating, depending upon how well it was applied, can begin to show wear after a year. Typically, it will have to be replated after three or four years.

Diamond Cuts

EMERALD-CUT: The most formal, rectangular stone, with 58 facets (mini-planes), cut with graduated "steps" or elongated side facets (which reflect like mirrors), and curved corners. The large, open facets make the color clearer.

HEART-SHAPED: A romantic variation of the pear-shaped stone, with the top silhouette resembling the top of a heart (similar to a sweetheart neckline).

MARQUISE: An oblong (boat-shaped) stone with 58 facets, a point on each end; large surface area for the carat weight that results in a longer look for fewer carats; named for a renowned marquise of her day, Madame de Pompadour, a duchess and the mistress of Louise XV.

OVAL: A variation of the round-cut stone; appears larger, more elongated than a round stone of equal carat weight; with 58 facets.

PEAR-SHAPED: A teardrop-shaped stone with 58 facets, pointed on one end (point is worn toward the fingernail), round on the other end; a cross between a round (brilliant) and a marquise cut.

PRINCESS: A square or rectangular cut with sharp, squared corners, 50 or 58 facets; an upside-down pyramid that is cut with most of the carat weight in the pavilion (bottom part of the stone); smallest of the shapes cut within the same carat weight.

ROUND (BRILLIANT): The traditional and most popular diamond cut, with 58 facets that maximize brilliance, reflecting more light than any other stone shape.

TRILLION: A triangular, avant-garde cut first seen in the late 1970s, with equilateral sides that are cut shallow and appear large for their carat weight; a beautiful brilliance.

WEDDING RING SHOPPING WORKSHEET (CIRCLE YOUR FINAL CHOICE)

Jewelry Store Name:		Phone no:				
Address:		E-mail:				
		Web site:				

Item:	Description:	Cost:	Order Date:	In stock/ order:	Comments

Jewelry Store Name:		Phone no:				
Address:		E-mail:				
		Web site:				

Item:	Description:	Cost:	Order Date:	In stock/ order:	comments

Select Bridal Jewelry

Pearls. The wedding ring is not the only piece of jewelry that is traditionally present at weddings. A pearl necklace and earrings have been a bridal custom since medieval times, and possibly earlier.

Jewelry was a popular gift for aristocratic medieval brides, who wore hair ornaments, coronals, and hair bands decorated with pearls and other gems. By the late fifteenth century, crowns were replaced with elaborate headdresses, called "crowns of marriage." Beginning in the Middle Ages, poor brides could rent marriage crowns and parures (an ensemble of matching necklace, earrings, hair comb, pin, and bracelet) from the local church or town hall to wear on her wedding day. This custom of renting bridal jewelry from the town survived well into the nineteenth century in Europe. Interestingly, this practice has been rejuvenated here in the U.S. with a modern-day twist: a number of Internet sites offer high-end jewelry rental for weddings.

The custom of giving pearls to brides, and of brides wearing pearl necklaces and earrings on their wedding day, has continued through modern times. In the 1950s, Prince Rainier of Monaco pledged his love to Grace Kelly with a necklace and earrings of pearls and diamonds. Seed-pearl embroidery on wedding gowns has become a bridal tradition, although today the pearls tend to be made of glass, resin, or even plastic.

Today, natural pearls are all but extinct because of water pollution. The only natural pearls available to modern brides are sold at estate jewelry sales. In 1920, Japanese Kokichi Mikimoto created a patented process that enabled the production of great numbers of round, lustrous pearls, which involves inserting

TIPS FOR PEARL MAINTENANCE

Each time you wear cultured pearls, wipe them down with a fine cloth to get rid of any perfume, cosmetics, or dirt. Store them in a jewelry box or flannel bag. Take them to your jeweler to be restrung and cleaned at least once a year.

a mother-of-pearl bead (made from the shell of a freshwater American mollusk) and a piece of mantle from one oyster into another oyster. Mikimoto also developed a grading system for pearls, which today is the industry standard.

To calculate the price of a pearl, first the pearl is weighed. The weight in grains is then multiplied by the base price, which depends on the shape, color, luster, and surface appearance of the pearl. Poor-quality pearls are assigned a C rating, followed by B, A, AA, AAA, Fine, and Gem. Some companies have instituted in-between grades, such as A+. Most of the pearls sold in the United States are graded A+ or AA.

Colored Gemstones. A gemstone, such as sapphire, emerald, or ruby, can add a touch of sparkling color to your otherwise all-white wedding day look. Also, you may prefer the colored gemstone pendants, earrings, or a tie tack or pair of cufflinks for the groom to the more traditional diamonds and pearls. When purchasing gemstone jewelry, color is the principal determinant of value, and the closer a colored gemstone comes to being the pure spectral hue of that color, the better. If the gem has the tag "precious" in the name, then be prepared to spend more.

With today's technology, it is possible to enhance colored gemstones in a variety of ways. Still, one of the most commonly encountered and commercially accepted methods of enhancement is the use of heat. The process of applying heat may lighten, darken, or completely change the color of the gemstone. The color obtained is usually permanent and the process is performed on rubies, sapphires, and the like.

Finally, get a certification of origin for the gemstone, especially if it has a geographical name attached to it. This authentication is important because gemstones have been sold in the past as if they were more valuable and of a higher grade than they actually were.

Swarovski Crystals. Brides who want to add sparkle without the expense of diamonds have a fabulous option with Swarovski crystal jewelry. Dating back to Austria, 1895, Swarovski cut-glass crystals came into the forefront in 1976, when the Silver Crystal Mouse was created for the Winter Olympics. A year later, the company entered the fashion and jewelry market. Today, Swarovski necklaces, pendants, earrings, bracelets, and pins are available to brides in a variety of styles and price points. (Even wedding gowns are embellished with the crystals.) And with so many options, they are not only a lovely way to enhance the bride but also the bridesmaids' ensembles.

Mail Your Invitations

Several months ago you considered all your stationery needs and ordered your invitations. Now is the time to finalize all the additional details — such as addressing envelopes and selecting stamps — before sending them on their way. If you are planning to use e-stationery, your vendor should have detailed instructions to walk you through digitally sending your invitations. The following checklist will help you with the final preparations if you are mailing traditional printed invitations.

INVITATIONS CHECKLIST

- ○ Mail wedding invitations no later than four to six weeks prior to the wedding, eight weeks in advance if during a holiday weekend

- ○ Visit the philatelic desk at your local post office or visit the Web site of the U.S. Postal Service (www.usps.com) to check out stamps that will personalize your invitations in a meaningful way for you and your fiancé (i.e., the breast-cancer research stamp, varied love-themed stamps, etc.)

- ○ Take a sample invitation, fully stuffed with both envelopes and all enclosures, to the post office to weigh — before buying and stamping. Many invitations require extra postage

- ○ Write/print the return address in the front, upper left-hand corner of the larger, outer envelope (with the "gummed" flap), as per U.S. Postal Service specifications

- ○ Before inserting each invitation, fold it across the middle of the engraved double card/sheet (unless printed on a flat card); insert it, folded side down, into the smaller, inside envelope (with the "ungummed" flap); the parent's (s') name(s) should be immediately visible when the flap is opened. (Single sheets should be slipped into the smaller, inside envelope with the "ungummed" flap, with the engraved side facing up.)

- ○ Position enclosure cards/maps/directions directly underneath the invitation (or inside the fold of the invitation)

- ○ The thin sheet of tissue paper (originally inserted to blot excess ink from early printing presses and keep letters from smudging and/or bleeding through to all other sheets and envelopes) can be discarded. If you do want to follow tradition, however, gently lay (or leave) each sheet of tissue directly on top of the printed side of each invitation

- ○ Allow extra weeks in your ordering time frame if you plan to hire a calligrapher to address each invitation. (Ask your calligrapher how much time he/she will need to complete your invitations, and order your envelopes/stationery/invitations early.)

- ○ When addressing smaller, inside envelopes (with "ungummed" flaps), include titles and surnames only. (See page 47)

- ○ When addressing larger, outer envelopes (with gummed flaps), include full names of guests

- ○ Insert the smaller, inside envelope into the outer, larger envelope, so that the guests' names (titles and surnames) are seen as soon as the outer envelope is opened

- ○ Seal the outer envelopes and apply stamps

Learn to Dance

One of the most romantic — and sentimental — moments at a wedding reception is the couple's first dance. A close second is the bride's dance with her dad.

Unfortunately, many couples today simply do not know how to ballroom dance. To make a beautiful impression on the dance floor, now is the time to sign up for some lessons.

The waltz is an easy dance to begin with. Its basic box step provides a nice foundation for many other dance steps. Couples who prefer not to have an old-fashioned, traditional dance, though, are creating fun and exciting alternatives for their guests to enjoy.

A dance teacher can choreograph a special dance for the two of you. This can be in the form of hip hop, country, rock, or pop routines. Guests are usually taken aback by the performance, as it's unexpected and unique. You may even want to involve the entire bridal party (think *Thriller*). Practicing the dance routine frequently will help you get the steps down. As you become more comfortable on your feet, you will feel more at ease improvising steps to different kinds of music.

DANCE LESSONS WORKSHEET (CIRCLE YOUR FINAL CHOICE)

School Name:		Phone no:	
Address:		E-mail:	
		Web site:	

Cost	Times	Dances Taught	

School Name:		Phone no:	
Address:		E-mail:	
		Web site:	

Cost	Times	Dances Taught	

School Name:		Phone no:	
Address:		E-mail:	
		Web site:	

Cost	Times	Dances Taught	

School Name:		Phone no:	
Address:		E-mail:	
		Web site:	

Cost	Times	Dances Taught	

Two Months Ahead

TASKS:

- ○ Compile your program book
- ○ Plan and book the ceremony rehearsal and dinner
- ○ Keep up with thank-you notes

TOOLS:

- ○ Program Book Planner
- ○ Ceremony Rehearsal Planning Worksheet
- ○ Rehearsal Dinner Planning Worksheet
- ○ Wedding Gift Organizer

Compile Your Program Book

With the technological advances that have happened in the printing industry and in desktop publishing in the past few years, printing up program books and pew cards is no longer as difficult and time-consuming as it used to be. But with so much still to be done for the wedding, it is wise to get as much of the printing done in advance as possible.

Your program book will serve as a memento of your special day. A nice touch is to print the cover on a beautiful decorative paper, and then to tie a ribbon, elastic thread, or cording around the middle of the booklet to give it a special flourish. Another way to go is to match it to your wedding invitations, by selecting the same or coordinating paper, lettering, and colors. Or, match the program to your overall wedding theme. If you're having a beach-themed wedding, for instance, the program might be die-cut in the shape of a shell. Be creative and don't hesitate to add personal information to the program, such as a special photograph or meaningful quotation. This is a nice keepsake for both of you and your guests.

By now you should have a clear idea of:

- Who is performing the ceremony

- Where it will be held

- Who your wedding party members are

- Which musicians will be playing at your ceremony

- The structure of the ceremony

- Highlights of the ceremony, such as a song or a poem to be read

These are the items to include in your ceremony program book, along with any special remembrances, messages, or thank-yous.

PROGRAM BOOK PLANNER

Program books are usually printed and bound in signatures of four pages each, so your book will always have an even number of pages. However, there is no rule that says your program book can't be as simple as one two-sided page. To determine the size, first list all of the ceremony contents. Then separate them in chronological order and space them out on pages. List the contents of each page of your program book on the lines to the left of the square boxes, below. Use the boxes to sketch graphic ideas or play with color.

Length of book:

Front cover:

Contents:

Page 1 contents: _____

_____

_____

_____

_____

_____

_____

Page 2 contents: _____

_____

_____

_____

_____

_____

_____

Page 3 contents: _____

_____

_____

_____

_____

_____

_____

Page 4 contents:

_____

_____

_____

_____

_____

_____

Page 5 contents:

_____

_____

_____

_____

_____

_____

Page 6 contents:

_____

_____

_____

_____

_____

_____

Program Book Planner Continued

Page 7 contents:

_____

_____

_____

_____

_____

_____

Page 8 contents:

_____

_____

_____

_____

_____

_____

Back cover contents:

_____

_____

_____

_____

_____

_____

Plan and Book the Ceremony Rehearsal and Dinner

Now is a good time to begin planning the rehearsal for the ceremony. You booked the ceremony site several months ago, but confirm that all is set for the run-through. The rehearsal dinner usually follows the rehearsal and it will be the perfect time for both of you to kick back a little and relax before all the wonderful craziness of the following momentous day.

Book a private room in a restaurant or banquet hall as they are usually the best place for a rehearsal dinner, although a family member can certainly host it at home for a more intimate evening. Traditionally, the groom's family hosted the rehearsal dinner. However, today it is not unusual for the bride's family or even the couple themselves to host this party.

Invitations should be mailed now and can be in the style of other wedding announcements (the engagement, for example), although it's perfectly acceptable for them to be less formal.

You don't need to hire a photographer to capture the rehearsal dinner, but do have cameras on hand so guests can snap candid shots. You might also want to designate someone to shoot video, so that all of the fun are forever part of your memories.

A GIFT FOR THE BRIDE OR GROOM

The custom of brides and grooms exchanging gifts with one another in commemoration of their wedding is a lovely wedding tradition. The gift should be long-lasting and have sentimental value for the receiver. It does not have to be expensive.

CEREMONY REHEARSAL PLANNING WORKSHEET

Every member of the wedding from the bridesmaids to the groomsmen, the ring bearers and flower girls and the musicians should attend this event. It's worth it for both of you to take time before the rehearsal to review the entire process. Use the Wedding Day Itinerary on page 241 for examples from a traditional wedding on the order of entry and exit. If all participants arrive on time, the rehearsal should take about an hour.

REHEARSAL TIME:

DATE:

LOCATION:

ITEMS I NEED TO BRING WITH ME (E.G., "FAKE" BOUQUET, READINGS, RING-BEARER PILLOW, ETC.):

WHO SHOULD ATTEND:

REHEARSAL DINNER PLANNING WORKSHEET

The guest list for the rehearsal dinner includes all members of the wedding party, the officiant and his or her spouse, and any close friends or family members who will attend the rehearsal.

REHEARSAL DINNER TIME:	
DATE:	
LOCATION:	

WHO SHOULD ATTEND:	
COST PER PERSON:	

Keep Up with Thank You Notes

If you haven't already, you soon will start to receive wedding gifts. Thank you notes should be sent as soon as possible after the gift arrives, and no later than eight weeks after its receipt. Since the next few months will be busy, take time now to stock up on some beautiful cards or fine stationery in a neutral color, pens, and stamps so you have them at your disposal whenever you need to write a thank-you. (If you can, match the thank you cards to the wedding invitation and other stationery you've ordered, for a cohesive look). If you are short on time, you could send a card custom-printed with a special thank-you message, and follow up with a personal note at some point; however, guests may take offense at a note that is not personally handwritten by one of you. If you are organized, a handwritten note shouldn't take but a few minutes of your time. Write from the heart, and mention the specific gift, and tell the reader how much you will enjoy using it. By the way, this is one task both of you should do together!

WEDDING GIFT ORGANIZER

NAME	GIFT DESCRIPTION	THANK YOU CARD SENT/DATE

WEDDING GIFT ORGANIZER

NAME	GIFT DESCRIPTION	THANK YOU CARD SENT/DATE

NAME	GIFT DESCRIPTION	THANK YOU CARD SENT/DATE

WEDDING GIFT ORGANIZER

NAME	GIFT DESCRIPTION	THANK YOU CARD SENT/DATE

WEDDING GIFT ORGANIZER

NAME	GIFT DESCRIPTION	THANK YOU CARD SENT/DATE

WEDDING GIFT ORGANIZER

NAME	GIFT DESCRIPTION	THANK YOU CARD SENT/DATE

WEDDING GIFT ORGANIZER

NAME	GIFT DESCRIPTION	THANK YOU CARD SENT/DATE

WEDDING GIFT ORGANIZER

NAME	GIFT DESCRIPTION	THANK YOU CARD SENT/DATE

NAME	GIFT DESCRIPTION	THANK YOU CARD SENT/DATE

WEDDING GIFT ORGANIZER

NAME	GIFT DESCRIPTION	THANK YOU CARD SENT/DATE

WEDDING GIFT ORGANIZER

NAME	GIFT DESCRIPTION	THANK YOU CARD SENT/DATE

WEDDING GIFT ORGANIZER

NAME	GIFT DESCRIPTION	THANK YOU CARD SENT/DATE

WEDDING GIFT ORGANIZER

NAME	GIFT DESCRIPTION	THANK YOU CARD SENT/DATE

WEDDING GIFT ORGANIZER

NAME	GIFT DESCRIPTION	THANK YOU CARD SENT/DATE

WEDDING GIFT ORGANIZER

NAME	GIFT DESCRIPTION	THANK YOU CARD SENT/DATE

One Month Ahead

TASKS:

○ Plan your wedding day itinerary

○ Organize the reception seating chart

○ Apply for a marriage license

TOOLS:

○ Wedding Day Itinerary Worksheet

○ Reception Seating Chart Planner

○ Three Weeks in Advance Task List

○ Two Weeks in Advance Task List

○ One Week in Advance Task List

○ The Day Before Task List

○ On the Day of the Wedding Task List

Plan Your Wedding Day Itinerary

We've provided a sample of a wedding day itinerary using 6pm as the ceremony time. The timetable is based on the bride and the wedding party being about 10 or 15 minutes away from the wedding ceremony site; adjust if the distance is longer. Also, be sure to ask your vendors (hair, makeup, florist, caterer, driver, photographer, etc.) what they recommend in terms of timing. These are suggestions, but we do know that often things can take longer than expected; the important thing for both of you is to find a few moments of quiet before the ceremony; take some deep breaths and relax.

Create your own itinerary using the grid provided on pages 242-243.

SAMPLE WEDDING DAY ITINERARY

TIME	EVENT
11am	• bridesmaids brunch or lunch
1pm	• bride and bridesmaids have their hair done
2:30pm	• bride and bridesmaids have their makeup done
4pm	• flowers arrive at ceremony site • photographer arrives at bride's location • bride and bridesmaids get dressed
4:30pm	• flower girl and ring bearer arrive at bride's location • groom and groomsmen dress
5pm	• officiant and ceremony musicians arrive at ceremony site
5:15pm	• prelude music begins and guests start to arrive
5:20pm	• transportation arrives at bride's location for pick up
5:30pm	• groom and groomsmen arrive at ceremony site • videographer arrives at ceremony site and sets up
5:35pm	• first round of transportation arrives at ceremony site with mother of the bride, flower girl, ring bearer, and bridesmaids
5:40pm	• the bride and father of the bride depart for the ceremony site
5:50pm	• the grandmothers of the bride and groom are escorted down the aisle • the mother of the bride, flower girl, ring bearer, and bridesmaids arrive at the ceremony site • the mother of the groom is escorted down the aisle
5:55pm	• the bride and father of the bride arrive at the ceremony site
5:57pm	• the groom and groomsmen line up at the top of the aisle
5:58pm	• the mother of the bride is escorted down the aisle
6pm	• processional music and bridal processional begins
6:45pm	• the ceremony ends and the recessional begins
6:50pm	• the ceremony receiving line is formed
7pm	• caterer arrives at reception location
7:30pm	• photographs are taken at specified location • cocktails and music begin at reception location
7:50pm	• the reception receiving line with bride, groom, and parents begins
7:55pm	• the best man or emcee present the bride and groom to the guests
8pm	• dinner is served
8:45pm	• speeches and toasts begin
9pm	• first dance of the bride and groom
9:30pm	• the wedding cake cutting ceremony
10:30pm	• bouquet toss
11pm	• bride and groom have their last dance of the evening
11:15pm	• bride and groom depart
midnight	• musicians pack up and leave

YOUR WEDDING DAY ITINERARY

TIME	EVENT

YOUR WEDDING DAY ITINERARY

TIME	EVENT

With the exception of the head tables, which tend to be rectangular, most tables sit six, eight, or ten people for dinner. (Cocktail tables tend to be much smaller, seating two to four people. But you do not need a seating plan for cocktails.) Ask your banquet hall director how many tables are planned and how many people can be seated at each table. Male and female guests usually alternate seating.

GUEST #	TABLE #	SEAT #	GUEST NAME
1			
2			
3			
4			
5			
6			
7			
8			
9			
10			
11			
12			
13			
14			
15			
16			
17			
18			
19			
20			

RECEPTION SEATING CHART PLANNER

GUEST #	TABLE #	SEAT #	GUEST NAME
21			
22			
23			
24			
25			
26			
27			
28			
29			
30			
31			
32			
33			
34			
35			
36			
37			
38			
39			
40			
41			
42			
43			
44			

RECEPTION SEATING CHART PLANNER

GUEST #	TABLE #	SEAT #	GUEST NAME
45			
46			
47			
48			
49			
50			
51			
52			
53			
54			
55			
56			
57			
58			
59			
60			
61			
62			
63			
64			
65			
66			
67			
68			

RECEPTION SEATING CHART PLANNER

GUEST #	TABLE #	SEAT #	GUEST NAME
69			
70			
71			
72			
73			
74			
75			
76			
77			
78			
79			
80			
81			
82			
83			
84			
85			
86			
87			
88			
89			
90			
91			
92			

RECEPTION SEATING CHART PLANNER

GUEST #	TABLE #	SEAT #	GUEST NAME
93			
94			
95			
96			
97			
98			
99			
100			
101			
102			
103			
104			
105			
106			
107			
108			
109			
110			
111			
112			
113			
114			
115			
116			

RECEPTION SEATING CHART PLANNER

GUEST #	TABLE #	SEAT #	GUEST NAME
117			
118			
119			
120			
121			
122			
123			
124			
125			
126			
127			
128			
129			
130			
131			
132			
133			
134			
135			
136			
137			
138			
139			
140			

GUEST #	TABLE #	SEAT #	GUEST NAME
141			
142			
143			
144			
145			
146			
147			
148			
149			
150			
151			
152			
153			
154			
155			
156			
157			
158			
159			
160			
161			
162			
163			
164			

RECEPTION SEATING CHART PLANNER

GUEST #	TABLE #	SEAT #	GUEST NAME
165			
166			
167			
168			
169			
170			
171			
172			
173			
174			
175			
176			
177			
178			
179			
180			
181			
182			
183			
184			
185			
186			
187			
188			

RECEPTION SEATING CHART PLANNER

GUEST #	TABLE #	SEAT #	GUEST NAME
189			
190			
191			
192			
193			
194			
195			
196			
197			
198			
199			
200			
201			
202			
203			
204			
205			
206			
207			
208			
209			
210			
211			
212			

Reception Seating Arrangements

SWEETHEART TABLE SEATING

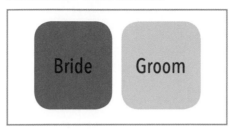

TRADITIONAL HEAD TABLE SEATING

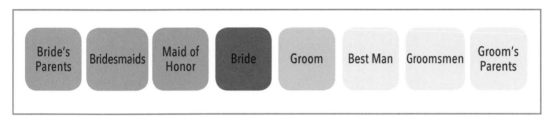

(If Jewish, the bride and groom switch places.)

INFORMAL HEAD TABLE SEATING

Apply for a Marriage License

A marriage license is a legal document that authorizes you to get married. Apply for your marriage license in the town, state, or country where you want to be married; sometimes, there is a wait of a few days before you receive the license. Some states and/or countries also require an additional waiting period before you can get married.

In the United States, the minimum age for marriage without parental consent is eighteen; be sure to check the laws in the country where you will marry as they vary. A driver's license can be used to provide proof of age. If you are marrying in the U.S., apply at the courthouse in the county in which you are getting married, unless otherwise directed by a town official.

In some states, both of you must appear in person at the courthouse to apply. No witnesses are necessary. Some states require blood test results from your physician in order to secure a marriage license. There is an application fee, and the waiting period before the license can be received is seventy-two hours. Once issued, the license remains valid for thirty days to a year, depending on the state. Anyone may pick up the license. For second marriages, a divorce decree (at least thirty days old) or proof of death is required.

Call your local county courthouse or municipal office well in advance of your wedding date for more information. If you are planning a civil service, call to find out who is available to perform the ceremony and the fees involved. The person who performs the ceremony is responsible for filing the license, blood test results, and marriage certificate after the wedding with the Registrar (or other appropriate official) of the county in which the ceremony took place. Be sure to follow up and verify that this has been done to avoid any problems in the future.

The Marriage Certificate

Just after your wedding ceremony, you, your spouse, the person who officiated, and one or two witnesses, will sign the marriage certificate.

Within a few days of your wedding, the person who married you will file the marriage certificate with the appropriate county official (depending on the state, this may be the registrar, clerk, or recorder). Depending on where you live, you will then be sent a certified copy of this certificate two weeks or so after you're married, or you will have to go and pick it up. The certified document you receive is your official proof of marriage.

It's always a good idea to check with the county clerk's office in the town you plan to marry for the up-to-date policy on marriage certificates. The location of your marriage will decree the look of your official marriage certificate, but as a special commemorative gesture, consider a custom marriage certificate created by a master calligrapher. Another option is a custom marriage certificate ornamented with decorative cutouts or small strips of paper rolled into decorative effects called quilling.

THE KETUBAH

The custom of the ketubah is surely one of the longest-standing of the ornamental marriage certificates. For 2,000 years, the Hebrew word ketubah has been used to refer to the certificate that Jewish law required to document a wedding. Perhaps the original prenuptial agreement, the ketubah was a legal and financial agreement that spelled out the groom's responsibilities to the bride, establishing and enumerating a financial contract between the parties, including the dowry. But ketubot are more than just matter-of-fact business documents; hand-lettered and decorated with colorful designs, they acknowledge the celebratory aspect of God's commandment.

It's all coming together now; the months of organizing and planning have paid off. Here's your week-by-week guide to the remaining details.

Three Weeks Ahead:

○ Arrange for any final alterations and for gown pickup or delivery.

○ Confirm that attendants have picked up outfits and that they fit.

○ Confirm that groomsmen have complete attire.

○ Book a hair and makeup practice session (bring headpiece).

○ Book a hair and makeup session for yourself and attendants (if necessary) for the wedding day.

○ Review honeymoon plans, tickets, passport, luggage etc.

Two Weeks Ahead:

○ Write rehearsal dinner speeches

○ Confirm booking for rehearsal dinner.

○ Contact the caterer with final guest numbers, menu review, and seating arrangements.

○ Confirm out-of-town guest accommodations.

○ Visit the post office to arrange for mail to be held while on your honeymoon and, if necessary, to file change-of-address forms.

○ Trial run your wedding shoes at home.

One Week Ahead:

○ Prepare a travel itinerary, and deliver or e-mail it to appropriate people.

○ Prepare task cards for wedding-party members.

○ Write checks for final balances.

○ Write checks and put them in separate envelopes for the officiant, organist, and choir.

○ Contact the newspaper about your wedding announcement.

○ Call the bakery, and confirm cake delivery to reception hall.

○ Organize cash for gratuities in individual envelopes.

FEEDING THE CREW

If you are serving a meal to your guests at the reception, don't forget to include the musicians, photographer, videographer, wedding planner, day-of coordinator etc. It is not necessary to feed them the full wedding day meal; ask the caterer to make some sandwiches. Seat them in the back of the room and use the same table linens as elsewhere.

The Day Before:

- ○ Pick up the tuxedos or suits.

- ○ Get manicure and pedicure.

- ○ Assemble the bride's emergency kit (needle and thread, safety pins, aspirin, pantyhose, tissues, and so forth).

- ○ Attend your wedding ceremony rehearsal and dinner.

- ○ Review seating instructions and pew cards with ushers.

- ○ Designate a bridal party member to distribute service fees (officiant etc.).

On the Day of the Wedding:

- ○ Eat a good breakfast.

- ○ If you're not styling it yourself, have your hair and makeup done by a professional.

- ○ Accept delivery of flowers.

- ○ Welcome bridesmaids at home or in dressing room.

- ○ Get dressed.

- ○ Pose for pre-ceremony photographs.

- ○ Make an entrance!

STORE YOUR WEDDING GOWN SAFELY

If you want to preserve your gown for years down the road as an heirloom, consult someone familiar with textile preservation at a local museum to find out which cleaner will best preserve your gown. Whatever you do, do not take your precious gown to just any dry cleaner for preservation and storage. Do a quick online search to find qualified cleaners who will take special care of your gown. Ask if they use acid-free tissue paper. Unbleached muslin should also be used to protect the gown in its box. Once back in your hands, store the boxed gown in a dry space (avoid damp or moist basements), preferably in a cedar-lined chest or drawer.

Use this comprehensive master spreadsheet to record and tally all wedding costs once they have been finalized. Its convenient format will allow you to see, at-a-glance, the complete expenditures for your wedding and honeymoon

ITEM	12 MONTHS	11 MONTHS	10 MONTHS	9 MONTHS	8 MONTHS
PLANNING EXPENSES					
Wedding Planner					
Master of Ceremonies					
Photography (pp. 58-59)					
Entertainment/Music: *Rehearsal Dinner, Ceremony, Cocktail Party, Reception, Other Events* (pp. 86-89)					
Invitations (p. 48)					
Dance Lessons (p. 211)					
Other					
WEDDING ATTIRE					
Bridal Gown/Tuxedo (pp. 110-111)					
Bridesmaids's Dresses/ Groomsmen Attire (pp. 114-129)					
Wedding Ring (p. 204)					
Other					
COCKTAIL PARTY					
Site (pp. 26-27)					
Food, Service, and Liquor (pp. 26-27)					
Decor/Flowers (pp. 79, 147)					
Transportation					
Other					
REHEARSAL DINNER					
Site (p. 221)					
Food, Service, and Liquor (p. 221)					
Decor/Flowers (pp. 79, 147)					
Transportation					
Other					
CEREMONY					
Site					
Officiant (pp. 14-15)					
Decor/Flowers (pp. 79, 147)					
Programs/Pew Cards					
Wedding License/Marriage Certificate Fee					
Transporation					
Other					
RECEPTION					
Site (pp. 26-27)					
Food, Service, and Liquor (pp. 26-27)					
Decor/Flowers (pp. 79, 147)					
Wedding Cake (p. 151)					
Valet Parking/Transportation					
Other					
OTHER EVENTS					
Engagement Party, Bridesmaids' Lunch, Post-Wedding Party					
Site					
Food, Service, and Liquor					
Other					
HONEYMOON (pp. 186-187)					
MONTH TOTAL					

Tally the final cost information gathered from the worksheets throughout this book.

7 MONTHS	6 MONTHS	5 MONTHS	4 MONTHS	3 MONTHS	2 MONTHS	1 MONTH

GRAND TOTAL

NOTES

_____
_____
_____
_____
_____
_____
_____
_____
_____
_____
_____
_____
_____
_____
_____
_____
_____
_____
_____
_____
_____
_____
_____
_____

NOTES

_____

_____

_____

_____

_____

_____

_____

_____

_____

_____

_____

_____

_____

_____

_____

_____

_____

_____

_____

_____

_____

_____

_____

_____

_____

_____

_____

NOTES

NOTES

_____

_____

_____

_____

_____

_____

_____

_____

_____

_____

_____

_____

_____

_____

_____

_____

_____

_____

_____

_____

_____

_____

_____

_____

_____

_____

_____

_____

_____

_____

_____

_____

_____

Index

Page numbers in italic indicate checklists, worksheets, and other useful tools and tips for planning your wedding.

Photo Credits: